PSI SUCCESSFUL BUSINESS LIBRARY

SELLING SERVICES

MARKETING FOR THE CONSULTING PROFESSIONAL

*No tiresome storytelling,
only useful information*

PAUL O'NEIL

The Oasis Press®
Central Point, OR

Published by The Oasis Press®/PSI Research
© 1998 by Paul O'Neil

This publication is designed to provide accurate and authoritative information in regard to the subject matter covered. It is sold with the understanding that the author and publisher are not engaged in rendering legal, accounting, or other professional service. If legal advice or other expert assistance is required, the services of a competent professional person should be sought.
— from a declaration of principles jointly adopted by a committee of the American Bar Association and a committee of publishers.

Editor: Karen Billipp
Interior design: Eliot House Productions
Cover illustration and design: Steven Burns

Please direct any comments, questions, or suggestions regarding this book to:
    The Oasis Press®/PSI Research
    Editorial Department
    P.O. Box 3727
    Central Point, OR 97502

    (541) 479-9464
    (541) 476-1479 fax
    info@psi-research.com e-mail

The Oasis Press is a Registered Trademark of Publishing Services, Inc., an Oregon corporation doing business as PSI Research.

Library of Congress Cataloging-in-Publication Data
O'Neil, Paul, 1956—
  Selling services : marketing for the consulting professional ,/ Paul O'Neil.
    p. cm.
  Includes index.
  ISBN: 1-55571-461-7 (pbk.)
  1. Consultants–Marketing.   2. Selling.   I. Title.
HD69.C6054   1998
001'.068'8—dc21   98–44932
                                    CIP

Printed and bound in the United States of America
First Edition 10 9 8 7 6 5 4 3 2 1 0
Printed on recycled paper when available.

Table
of Contents

*"Put it before them briefly so they will
read it, clearly so they will appreciate
it and accurately so they will be
guided by its light."*
— JOSEPH PULITZER

Preface

New projects and new business opportunities are initially undefined. Your goal is to define and solve these situations. During this fact-finding and problem-solving process, you probably will be met with the challenge of changing people's perceptions. This requires professional selling skills. To be effective, you have to understand and anticipate all that can happen between you and your client. Additionally, you need to know how to make the right decisions on the fly and create the climate necessary to close business. The whole process is very definable. This book contains the skill and knowledge that are the basis of good selling. *Selling Services* is a comprehensive, technically organized, and concise business tool.

The first chapter introduces marketing plan creation and tactics for getting to your first client. The next three chapters cover one-on-one selling practice, persuasion, and negotiation, and include a very unique negotiation flow chart. The chart, supported by text, guides you through topic development and illustrates the tactical aspects of closing business. There are many solid examples that introduce these procedures for all types of situations. Summaries conclude each chapter. The fifth chapter could almost stand on its own. It includes a client profile strategy, field implementation plan, and a thorough description of how an experienced professional manages his or her client base of existing, new (target), large and small accounts. It also has information on forecasting, cost justification, price setting, winning competitive situations, proposals, bids, and example contractual relationships. The epilogue includes a final skills summary for your business.

Since graduating from University of California – Berkeley, I've been working in Northern California's Silicon Valley for several years as a Consulting Engineer and more recently as a technical services Marketing/Sales Manager. I've been very fortunate (and unfortunate) to have had a wide range of experiences that add to the scope of the selling topics you're about to read.

I'd like to thank Sydney J. Reuben (word processor and editor) and Lyon Ruthbun (writer and teacher) for their rhetorical input. I also wish to thank, for their advice and support, a few good friends and professionals with whom I have had "quality discussions."

Make a small investment and take with you the knowledge in this book.

"Lack of opportunity is often nothing more than lack of purpose or direction."

— UNKNOWN

CHAPTER ONE

Getting to Your First Client

A service business starts from some kind of initial catalyst. Outside the corporate environment, one finds people who simply start their business from scratch, with no contacts for leverage. And some start their business with only a basic skill set. Others buy a company or franchise with little knowledge of that particular business. When you look at today's corporate downsizing, you find many people with skills, who have developed many contacts. They may use this background to launch their own operations. A company may discontinue a line of business, where an individual employed by the company "inherits" that line of business. New clients, however, can be difficult to obtain. Word-of-mouth is powerful, but happens in its own time frame, which is usually not fast enough. Hence a start-up situation may generate immediate cash flow or none at all. Certainly, one needs clients for cash flow income. Therefore the business owner is often faced with doing some financial planning, marketing and sales, which he or she may have never previously done.

Business Plan

A business plan includes financial and marketing information. In addition to money for purchasing or expanding a business, you will need a positive cash flow to cover your ongoing overhead, expenses, and costs. If you can avoid borrowing money to start your business, fantastic. Typically, however, you may need more than you have set aside and will have to find a lender or lenders. Keep a close eye on how much debt you take on, because you will

---

Sample Outline of Business Plan

I. Business Description
Current Status
Experience
Mission Statement

II. Market Scope
History
Trends
Current Business Conditions

III. Market Segmentation

IV. Customer Base and Target Clients

V. Competition

VI. Sales Implementation
Selling Tactics
Priorities
Market Share Goals
Service/Support Strategy
Promotion
Delivery of Service

VII. Financials
Revenue Goals
Budget
Cash Flow Projections
Profit & Loss Projection

---

have to service that debt. Lenders can take the form of friends, family, or private investors.

If you have to go to a commercial bank, capital may be difficult to obtain. The bank may finance up to 50 percent of your needs and will want 100 percent collateral on their loan with a payback of three to five years. They will also want points over prime interest rate. You will have to show the bank that you have expertise in the field of business you are pursuing. If you are an existing business, banks like to see a few years of successful operation as a prerequisite for a loan. The Small Business Administration guarantees loans with more generous terms, financing up to 90 percent with several years' payback and low fees. Loan package requirements may specify a detailed business plan, which includes complete financial estimates, projections, and marketing plan. This can represent the minimum of information a lending institution may require.

One requirement for marketing would be to define what your typical client will look like functionally and how they would purchase and use your services. If you are leveraging your "old company" background in your new business, your market may look a little different from the one you worked within while at the company where you initially got your experience. Alternatively, if everything is new to you, thorough marketing homework is highly suggested before you start your business. It is critical to develop a written marketing plan. This will help you create and form your business concept. Since you are affected by market opportunities, competition, and limitations, you should describe your position in the market at well as your goals for the market. Writing a marketing plan will help you scrutinize your business and set better priorities for your overall business plan requirements. Use the Sample Outline of a Business Plan for a guide.

Marketing Plan

A marketing plan can stand on its own or be part of an overall business plan. Your marketing plan or outline should include details of prevailing economic conditions. What is going on with the economy that is helping or fighting you? How many different types of projects can you pursue as a business or how many market segments can you address? How much revenue is being or can be generated for each market segment for your geographical area of influence? How many competitors do you have? Is there anything unique, differentiating, or compelling about what you do vis-á-vis some of your competitors? Do you have a mission statement for yourself or your organization? What are the profiles of the types of clients you can approach for business? Is your bidding or pricing structure (margins) competitive for all the market segments you can address? Is revenue growth part of your agenda? What goals must you attain to reach the desired level of growth? What kind of budget and cash flow would you need? What ideas do you have for promotion? Are there any "business partners" you can team up with and leverage? After you have done due diligence to creating a plan and you have opened your doors for business, it is time to do some prospecting for new clients.

Prospecting

Prospecting on an ongoing basis will help ensure a constant flow of business opportunities. If you have existing accounts, you will have to prospect part of the same day you service these accounts. This is demanding, but if you schedule ahead you can do it. You will see more consistent cash flow and have a sense that you are doing something for tomorrow.

Realize that to land one client, you are going to make a handful of appointments. And to make a few appointments, you must contact several prospects because out of those several prospects, only a few will qualify for an appointment. And fewer will result in new business. Therefore prospecting is an activity you must quantify to ensure at least a reasonable income. Each type of business has its own trend regarding how many contacts lead to appointments, which lead to new business in a given time frame. For your business, know their relationship to each other.

During a given week, plan your activities for the following weeks. Of course, there is a limit to advance planning, as there is for your clients' ability to make plans in advance. Find out what this limit is and reach it.

Some prospects have the potential to become customers quicker than others. You need to prioritize who you contact. At the top of your list are your referrals from a satisfied customer. These people are pre-qualified in a sense and may not be far from becoming customers. They know your services. They know a happy client and have similar business needs. Some referrals come to you, but generally you have to ask for them. If you meet someone who likes your offering but does not qualify, ask for a referral. Get the referral's phone number, address, and some background on the referral's situation. In other words, do a little qualifying. These kinds of leads are gifts you cannot afford to neglect.

A second source of pre-qualified leads can come from the responses to your advertisements. People answer your ads for a reason. It may be just curiosity. If they do not qualify, ask for the referral. People know people who are in the same business or have similar interests.

Exchanging business leads with other sales and business people is another source of pre-qualified clientele. This practice has been termed "networking." Networking is hard to get off the ground; it is a marketing effort in itself. Begin by approaching businesses or people who do business with the same people you do business with. Meet with these people on a semi-regular basis. These people may be in a different type of business, although you will both be calling on the same people and organizations. For example, you may be an architect networking with a furniture salesperson. If you have a lead exchange program that generally produces similar results, great! If lead exchange is a one-way street, whereby you are the only one giving or receiving leads, offer cash rewards for sales you make as a result of leads given to you or request cash for the sales your contact makes from your leads. Nothing will be in writing, so network with people you trust.

Many prospective clients you contact will never have heard from you in the past. This situation has been termed "cold calling." Depending on your type of business, there are many published sources to pursue for lead generation. County and city directories, which are available to buy, contain a list of local commercial and industrial organizations with detailed information. We are now seeing more and more special directories of specific classifications. Some directories include nationwide coverage. You also have at your disposal Dunn & Bradstreet, Million Dollar Directory, Standard and Poore's Directory, and the Thomas Register of American Manufacturers. In addition, you have the Internet, where you can do a variety of searches for specific information.

Your industry trade magazines, with their business articles, calendar of events, press releases, advertising, and trade show announcements may be among your best sources of business lead information. Industry trends affect your strategies and priorities. Attend a few worthwhile trade shows. Get on those mailing lists. Investigate joining business organizations, social clubs, church groups where appropriate. Remember, you can't simply join organizations, show up a few times, and expect to receive significant benefits; they require the investment of time.

There are many aspects of doing business that do not entail direct contact with people, by phone or in person. Depending on your business, you want to make the most of the hours when people are available to be contacted. In most cases, these are business hours, five days per week. Because people have their own meetings, lunches, and administrative chores to attend to, you can only count on three hours in the morning and three hours in the afternoon for direct customer contact. This implies that you be well-organized and use your time wisely. Being well-organized in itself is not enough. In other words, you can be well-organized and still take care of tasks at the wrong time. Therefore you want to prioritize your activities. We are speaking of a knowledge of what to do among a choice of activities and when to expedite them. This is often called time management. There are many books and audio tapes available on this subject. Good time management requires discipline and on-going vigilance.

As a service provider, you act as a consultant; you are asking questions, uncovering problems previously unknown, helping establish priorities, clarifying long-range thinking, advocating, and persuading. Direct customer contact involves selling. Depending on the type of service you may offer, a great deal of selling still may be required to be successful, or simply a moderate level of selling skill may be all that is necessary. If you are consulting for a specific application or solution, where the need is fairly obvious, a moderate level of selling skill may be required. This has been termed "aware need selling." You are bringing your service to the attention of someone who already has a need for it. If your offering is a commodity, where your services are used repeatedly, then the relationship with your client may be most important; personality compatibility may become a dominant factor in maintaining your business relations. This has been termed "relationship selling." If your consulting involves a broad or systematic area, where only after reviewing client goals, objectives, and current situation do the needs become clear, only then can solutions be designed. This has been termed "unaware need selling" and requires a high degree of selling skill.

It is time to begin the selling process.

> *"Progress is the sum of small victories won by individual human beings."*
> — BRUCE CATTON

Summary

1. Take the time to write the best marketing plan possible.

2. After goals, priorities, and limitations are established, create a business plan.

3. Prospect for new clients on a consistent and on-going basis. Prioritize who you contact first. Referrals should be at the top of your list. Lead exchange networking is a good way to leverage your time. Advertising and special purpose directories are another source for potential clients.

4. Managing your time for the execution of action items during and after hours is also important. Provide yourself with a mix of daily activities; make sure new business efforts are not left out of your daily activities.

"Everyone lives by selling something."

— ROBERT LOUIS STEVENSON

CHAPTER TWO

Your Selling Initiation

Professional selling is an important part of the consultation process. You are selling when you introduce new information to a client. You are selling when you change a client's perception. And you are selling when you help a client make decisions. Professional selling is not rushing people to decisions without adequate consulting and disclosure of information: The connotation of "being sold" does not fit the description of professional selling. This book is not about "being sold." Then what is selling? Is it a persuasive attitude? That is indeed part of the selling equation. However, selling involves not only a persuasive attitude, but a definable procedure for communication which in itself is persuasive. This procedure consists of various kinds of questions.

The Critical Use of Questions

How does the consultant discover all the information necessary to help a client make appropriate decisions? He or she does this through the use of questions. Above all, you must listen carefully to the answers. Answers to questions not only provide you with factual information, they also yield the client's agreement or disagreement with respect to you and your services. Answers to questions tell you what kinds of questions to ask next. Hence questions give you interview control and direction. There are basically two types of questions:

1. fact-finding questions

2. agreement questions

Fact-Finding Questions

After your introduction to the prospective client, begin asking fact-finding questions; the purpose is to learn about the person's business situation as it may relate to your offering. Fact-finding questions fall into two categories:

1. general fact-finding questions
2. specific fact-finding questions

Begin with general fact-finding questions. General questions break the ice and allow information to flow from any area of concern the client may have. In a given situation one may begin with a question like, "How does your testing procedure work here, John?" This question gives John plenty of flexibility to discuss his testing procedures. Specific questions are used to elicit specific information. One might ask a specific question like, "Who designed this bridge, Karen?" Karen can respond with only one answer.

As you ask these kinds of questions, you will soon realize whether you are dealing with a talkative person or an unresponsive person. If lots of information comes flying your way, you'll have to direct the client into the areas you want to explore. You do this with your specific fact-finding questions.

Alternatively, you may be getting very little response from your general fact-finding questions. Therefore begin to use some specific fact-finding questions to get specific answers. To avoid sounding like an interrogation expert while asking specific questions, you can soften your questions by occasionally offering the client a choice.

Consultant: Did you seismically retrofit this structure or was it totally rebuilt?

Client: We had to rebuild it.

Fact-finding questions, general or specific, can be worded to yield a simple "yes" or "no" answer from the client. The purpose of this type of question is to get information the client will not think of or want to offer. This type of question should be used after you are well into your fact finding. Suppose you do have some information regarding the client's business from your general and specific fact-finding questions, but you still are not making much progress. At this point, if you feel you can verify problem areas, try asking a related fact-finding question which will yield a "yes" or "no." This may be your only hope for progress.

Consultant:	How do you like your control system for your wastewater treatment facility, Mr. Jones?
Client:	Okay, it does the job.
Consultant:	Who installed your control system?
Client:	Perfect Controls, Inc.
Consultant:	And does it handle all inputs of your algorithm?
Client:	It's supposed to.
Consultant:	I'm very familiar with your system, Mr. Jones. It is a good one. However, Mr. Jones, are you experiencing some false alarms?
Client:	Well, yes, I am.

In this example, the consultant's last two questions were designed to reveal a problem which the client could have been facing. The consultant knew from the client's answers to previous questions, and from visual inspection, that the client's existing alarm system was not installed properly. Therefore the consultant had the confidence to ask that last specific fact-finding question, worded to yield a yes or no, which was designed to verify the existence of a problem. Had the consultant known nothing of the client's alarm system, he or she would have simply been taking a pot shot at the client. After an introduction, suppose a consultant asked questions like these:

Consultant:	Would you like to invest in the best control software available?
Client:	No.
Consultant:	Is that portable unit rather heavy for your field use?
Client:	No, it's fine.

The effect is obvious. Before uncovering any hidden facts which might cause the client to like the idea of investigating software ownership or lighter field equipment, the consultant blindly asked fact-finding questions which yielded a "yes" or a "no." Such an approach usually leaves the consultant with useless, vague information.

As you begin to reveal potential problems the client may be facing, you will want to verify the client's agreement of the existence of that problem or problems. As a matter of fact, any time you introduce a new idea or information to your client which is intended for his or her benefit, verify if the client agrees with that idea or information. This is a key part of your persuasion process. If the client does not agree, you may have to do more fact-finding, more problem-solving, or a better job of phrasing your questions.

Agreement Questions

The verification of the client's agreement involves the second type of question, the agreement question. How do you use an agreement question? You introduce new ideas to the client in question form by adding words to the sentence which request their agreement. This type of question always generates a "yes" or "no" answer.

1. Those false control alarms can sure be aggravating, can't they?

2. Can you see where our approach to control will secure every point of the plant?

Generally, I prefer to place the words which ask for the agreement at the beginning of the question. But when you need to be extra effective, place those words at the end of the question, as in Question #1 above.

Questions can also be directed to you from the client. What if the client asks you a fact-finding question to probe for information? You have to be careful here; you want to control the flow of information in an orderly manner. Hence you need to discuss information which is only pertinent to helping the client solve a problem or enhance his or her situation. Clients may be simply curious and ask you questions that have little to do with their real needs. On the other hand, their question may be very pertinent. The point is that you do not know. To find out, answer the client's fact-finding question with a fact-finding question which yields a "yes" or "no" answer. In other words, treat it like a hot potato by returning the burden of answering the question to the client. A client may ask a consultant, "Do you use hydraulic equipment for installation?" Think about that. What difference does it make? That was a very specific question for a very practical application — installing equipment. So, with a little alarm going off in your mind, you ask, "Is hydraulic installation equipment what you require?" The client may very well respond, "Oh no, I was just wondering."

If the client asks a logical fact-finding question and you are at a very early stage of your consulting process, give him or her an answer and quickly follow with a fact-finding question. The client may ask, "Do you have your own subcontractors for construction?" You respond, "Yes" (if you can indeed provide them). You then quickly follow with, "What other approach might you be considering?" What you are doing here is giving the client an answer and getting a clearer idea of what he or she wants. Handling such a question in this manner helps the client to relax. If you simply answered "yes" or "no," you are dead in the water; you don't even know if the client is considering other options. Remember, you want interview control, not in a manipulative sense, but for information gathering.

Be careful about using the word "why" in your questioning process. Asking a client why they do something or think in a certain way is challenging. It forces the client to come up with a reason or rationale. If the client has a poor reason for doing something, it will be necessary to admit it. If the situation forces the client to lie, you may make an enemy out of your client. However, if you have the client well on your side and you feel you are ignorant of important facts relating to critical issues, go ahead and use "why." For example, "Why do you have your water treatment process set up the way you do, Fred?" Such a question might generate useful information. If you do use the question "why," always use it in sentence form. Avoid saying the word "why" by itself and never use "why" to express your disagreement with a client. Also, do not ask questions the client will not know how to answer. Here is an example of a consultant putting the client in an awkward position:

Consultant:	Did you realize that 50 percent of engineers have gone to digital printing?
Client:	No, I didn't. ... Hey, I bet a digital printout on standard sized 8½" x 11" paper would be convenient.
Consultant:	Now why would you want to do that?
Client:	Well, I . . . I don't know. It seemed reasonable.
Consultant:	Look! All you want is a narrow 2" x 2" strip chart, with any violation of high and low limits to be printed on it. A full report is a waste of print time and paper.

Never disagree with your client. A proper response to the client's suggestion would have been:

Consultant:	Mr. Adams, 50 percent of engineers have gone to digital printing.
Client:	Hey, I bet a digital printout on standard sized paper would be convenient.
Consultant:	Yes, it would. Or, you could simply use a narrow strip chart to print out any violation of high and low limits. Can you see where you would save on the quantity of paper you'd have to buy?

Don't flex your muscles with knowledge by degrading the client's lack of knowledge. Allow clients to express their ideas. Introduce your ideas carefully and with discretion. Competing with your client will only cause you trouble. Don't put yourself at this kind of unnecessary disadvantage. When clients give you a positive buying comment about your services, support it. Do this with a question which asks them to verify what they have just said:

> Client: Hey, I bet a digital printout would be convenient.

> Consultant: It sure would, wouldn't it?

What the consultant did was ask them an agreement question. When the client says "yes," you know you have his or her verification. You will also run into a situation where a client will ask you a question which would yield a "yes" or "no" answer to solicit your state of agreement to a point the client is trying to make. Here again, you have to be careful. If it clearly supports your position, simply agree. Otherwise, do not answer with a "no." You can clarify the point the client is trying to make by getting more information from him or her. Do this by making a statement or two which will allow you to ask more questions. For example, the client may say:

> Client: Yours and the other services out there are all the same, Mr. Consultant, so my decision is really going to be based on price, right?

> Consultant: Well, I can see how at first you might feel that way, Mr. Client. Let's investigate a few things about our approach which may shed new light on the situation.

Fact-finding questions, general or specific, and questions requesting a person's state of agreement are used throughout the entire consulting process.

In one sense, you, the consultant are initially way ahead of the client — you are approaching the client for a reason. To expect a new client to like you and to realize the benefits of your services right away is taking a lot for granted. When does the client's complete appreciation for your offering take place? Much of it may very well take place after that initial business decision, or long after your client becomes a customer. Appreciation for your offering by the customer can take place many times throughout the life of a project.

I bought a computer software package to help edit this book. When I was shopping for a word processing package, I didn't know which one would be the best for my application. All the consultants told me theirs was the package for me. I still didn't know what to do. However, one consultant showed me a testimonial from a computer magazine which matched one specific software package for editing and printing long documents. I still didn't know whether that software matched my requirements, but the consultant insisted it did. I bought the software. I was excited. But I still had doubts about my $200 investment, and about halfway through the instruction manual I thought, "What have I gotten myself into?" All my excitement was gone. Yet just two weeks later, after investing some time, I was very pleased with my decision. I was more excited than I had ever been during the whole experience. Hence as a consultant, not only are you leading the client to action, you are making decisions ahead of the client and for the client. This phenomenon exemplifies a part of the challenge and responsibility that exists in consultant-client relations.

When people first begin to consider a buying decision, they do so with an initial set of perceptions and reasons. Generally, you might know why people buy new services (unhappy with current provider, cost, quality), but initially you probably will not know the specific reasons. You, as the consultant, need to discover and clarify those specific reasons and their prioritization in the client's mind through the use of questions.

The Most Powerful Persuasion: What You Say and How You Say It

Along with your questions as tools of persuasion, let's briefly touch on the aspects of persuasion we usually accept as givens. The first impression experienced by an individual during an introduction is through the sense of sight. Obviously, you should be appropriately dressed. Appropriate dress implies dress similar to that of the people you deal with, which might include formal business or casual attire.

Greet the person with a slight smile. When you enter an office, wait until the other person sits down before you take a seat. Maintain good posture, whether sitting or standing. Movements made during any presentation or demonstration should be purposeful, relaxed, and kept to a minimum. Going into your briefcase too fast, too slowly, or too many times can be distracting. On the other hand, don't look like a store mannequin with rigid posture. Look relaxed, yet exhibit a mentally and physically alert state. Use body movement and facial expression in a persuasive manner. This might include the raising of an eyebrow or the slight movement of your hand. Again, time these movements to accent your presentation. Avoid body contact unless the client wants to shake your hand.

Your eye contact should be non-threatening, yet directed to the client. Don't give clients an exploratory stare. At first, let their eye contact be your guide. If they quickly glance at you now and then, you initially do the same. Catch their quick glance with your own, alternating with the client as to who looks away first. If you stare at your clients while they are obviously trying to avoid eye contact, you will upset them. Clients who look directly at you may be evaluating your reactions. Look back at them with a relaxed yet confident expression. Clients may stare at you. If you "stare right back," in a sense you are challenging them. Allow your clients that extra time to get comfortable with you.

The customer's sense of sound involves your voice and speech delivery. The sound of your voice should be pleasant and not too loud or soft. It too should have character, consisting of different tones and moderate voice inflections. Sounding monotone or like a perfect TV newscaster can upset the client. Speak at a moderate speed so the client can understand you. If you speak too fast, the client may distrust your intentions. Taking a public speaking course at a community college might be a wise idea if you feel you need the practice.

If you have a particularly strong vocabulary and the client does not, don't alienate the client with its use; simply speak as plainly as you can, maintaining the integrity of your message. Everything about your appearance, tone of voice, speech, body language, and the client's need for your service could be ideal; but if you use poorly chosen phrases, you can degrade everything you have going for you. For example, "Mr. Touché, adopting our solutions will remove that shackle around your neck and help you slide onto easy street. You'll be sold on this. Hurry, sign here!"

The whole point about appealing to a person's senses is to be non-threatening and non-patronizing. You want the client to be comfortable during your persuasion process. People may very well buy for a definite requirement of service, but their approach to accepting information for making a decision is emotional. When clients are emotionally fighting you, they will not work with you to see any intended benefits. They may not actually disagree with you, but they certainly won't agree with you.

> "He who can explain himself can command
> what he wants ... he who cannot is left in
> poverty."
>
> — GEORGE HERBERT PALMER

Summary

1. Begin with general fact-finding questions and gather your client information.

2. If the client is very talkative, gradually direct the flow of information by using specific fact-finding questions.

3. If the client is unresponsive, begin to use specific fact-finding questions to discover information.

4. At times, offer a client a choice when fact-finding.

5. If you are not discovering good information that would indicate a client need, carefully use fact-finding questions which yield a "yes" or "no" answer to discover motives.

6. Use agreement questions to verify the client's comprehension of new ideas.

7. Support the client's positive comments with agreement questions.

8. If the client asks you a question, be careful how you answer it. It helps to clarify the client's question with a question of your own. For the sake of efficiency, always strive to control the quality and direction of information.

9. Be careful about asking the question "why."

10. Use imagination to discover implications from the client information you gather.

11. Always consider the client's emotions. Utilize non-threatening expressions. Avoid being prejudged unfairly and inaccurately. Exhibit professionalism and confidence.

*"Experience is the hardest kind of teacher.
It gives you the test first and the lesson
afterward."*
— UNKNOWN

CHAPTER THREE

Qualification and Presentation, by Phone and in Person

What determines the qualification of a potential customer? Qualifying is a matter of determining whether or not clients can utilize your offering to enhance their process or situation in some way. If an individual strongly qualifies, it does not guarantee that he or she will become your customer. It is the consultant's challenge to turn a potential customer into a paying customer.

Qualification does require an investment of your time; it requires fact-finding, and is generally a two-stage evaluation. The first stage of client qualification is for the appointment. This is usually done on the telephone. Based on mostly technical information that you gather from a combination of marketing and this initial telephone call, you decide whether or not to invest the time and energy necessary to prepare for a meeting with the client. When you meet with the client, the second stage of qualification involves your "on the spot" analysis of just how beneficial your offering is or will be to the client. Don't forget that the client must be able to fund the offering. Attempt to discover anything that might prevent business as soon as possible. Poor qualification always leads to frustration. You do not have the time, energy, or money to waste. You have current customers to look after. If a potential client does not qualify, politely excuse yourself without closing the door on future opportunities.

You begin your fact-finding with a little pre-call research. You're not just calling anyone. You are approaching people who you think can use your services. Know something about the size of their company, number of employees, their markets, competitors, and types of projects they handle. Try to a copy of an annual report if you are selling to a corporation. These kinds of tidbits help you qualify before you ever speak to the client. Then from the information you gather, prepare a brief set of initial fact-finding questions. Such questions might include asking them what they are doing now with respect to the kind of service you have to offer. Or how they are using current services, how often they use them, and in what location services are being utilized. Verify your pre-call research with questions regarding the company. You want to determine the client's needs and whether or not you can meet those needs. If you can quickly determine whether an individual or company can become a customer, great. If not, you must dig for more information. Your ability to ask good questions implies sound knowledge of the potential customer applications. Along with your qualifying questions, prepare a brief presentation about yourself, your services, and your company.

Using the Telephone Skillfully

With our busy schedules and the benefits of telecommunications, your initial contact may well be made over the phone. Most people you call on will resist communicating over the telephone. The reasons vary. A major reason is that you will be a stranger to them. Because you're unknown your call may be assumed to be a low priority. They do not want to describe complex concepts or details to a stranger on the telephone. This is extra work. Their minds think, "Forget it," and they give you short and sometimes unclear, inaccurate answers. Others simply do not like talking business over the telephone. Some may be very busy and more inclined to deal with what is right in front of them.

When the client resists sharing information on the phone, you may feel rejection. And because your own direction with the client is unclear, or because you do not know how well he or she will qualify, you may not exude your enthusiasm when speaking with the client. You can't have much effect on others if you think about any potential problems or pitfalls you may encounter during an exchange. Concentrate only on your objectives. Treat each call as a new opportunity. Everything I said about appealing to the client's senses still holds — your tone of voice and speech delivery will reflect your professionalism.

The Role of the Receptionist

As a consultant, you will most likely be initiating most of your new business contacts by telephone. You will either have no idea who your contact will be or you will have a name from an advertising response or a referral. Unless you have a direct extension, probably the first person you'll talk to may be the receptionist. Part of the receptionist's job is to screen unfamiliar calls to protect employees from taking unwanted calls. The receptionist will ask you to leave a message or will ask you about the nature of your call before putting you through to anyone. If you ask for someone by name, you have a chance of being put through. If you do not have a name and you are an unfamiliar caller with a very common mission, the receptionist will evaluate the importance of your call as a low priority.

Alternatively, receptionists within larger organizations may not know to whom to connect you, and will not want to bother finding out. They do have a busy job. However, you have a job to do, too, don't you? Receptionists are not aware of all their company's and supervisor's needs. Never let a receptionist disqualify his or her company as a potential client, unless the company is small and the receptionist gives you a lot of information supporting his or her position.

With or Without a Contact Name

Suppose you do not have a contact name. As soon as the receptionist answers the phone, ask for a job title of the person who usually handles your offering. You might say, "The plant manager, please." If you do not know the exact title and the receptionist responds with a comment like, "He is very busy now and cannot take calls," you can respond, "Okay, may I send him a letter, please?" Upon the receptionist's affirmative reply, ask, "What is your mailing address, please?" After you are answered, very quickly add, "And to the attention of?" Ask for the address first, getting the receptionist's mind off the fact that you want a name. If the receptionist responds, "Send it to me," state that the information is very technical and confidential, and must be sent direct. If you are still refused, leave a message.

Use your imagination when trying to locate contacts within the larger organizations. If you have a name, your objective is to get the receptionist to put you through to the name you request. If you appeal to the receptionist's company interests and are polite, you can get the help you need. After the receptionist asks for your name, state who you are. Build familiarity by asking for and using the receptionist's name. Appeal to the person's company interests by stating why you are approaching the company.

You can also appeal to the receptionist's company interests by assuming that the company is actively seeking your offering. After all, you don't know if they are or not. The receptionist may not know either.

Consultant:	Yes, your name please?
Receptionist:	This is Ken. May I help you?
Consultant:	Yes, Ken. Gary Jones, please.
Receptionist:	What is this regarding?
Consultant:	I'm Dean Edwards with Structures in Place. I'd like to submit a bid for your new construction project. I'd like to speak with Gary Jones.
Receptionist:	What kind of information do you need? Maybe I can help you.
Consultant:	Well, Ken, when you take bids do you insist on the use of custom software or third-party packaged software?
Receptionist:	I'm sorry, Mr. Edwards, I have no idea.
Consultant:	No problem. Please go ahead and put me through to Gary, Ken. I have a few technical details I'd like to iron out.

Again, what Dean did here was request help. When the receptionist could not possibly comply, Dean was put through to the person who was requested as a source of knowledge. If you are not simply put through after requesting a name, the receptionist may have put you on hold while informing the contact of the nature of your call. If the receptionist comes back and says, "Dean, we are not taking bids at this time," the contact probably did not want to take the call.

When this happens and you feel there could be considerable business at stake, send the contact a letter in a nonstandard-sized, colored envelope. Mark it Personal and Confidential and the secretary might not take the liberty of opening the mail. In the letter, appeal to the internal contact's company goals. Include a testimonial on benefits you have delivered to similar clients in the recent past. State that you wish to discuss mutual business interests and end the letter by requesting that he or she accept your telephone call later in the week. Don't put much more information in the letter. The more you include, the more the contact can prejudge and object to. The goal of the letter is to get the contact to tell the receptionist, "Okay, I'll take the call."

(Alternatively, you may have been referred to an individual by someone else within the company. If not put through, mention that you were referred and by whom.)

Getting the Appointment

If you are put through to a contact you do not know, one of two things just happened: You were connected with a decision maker (this may be someone who can strongly influence the final decision or the person who actually says "yes" or "no") or you were connected with someone who might screen people for the decision maker(s). Initially, let's assume you are talking to a decision maker. Your next challenge is to get the internal contact's interest, get some information, and get the appointment. Again, pursue the appointment only if you feel the client qualifies for a visit. Because you are talking to a possibly influential contact with whom you may be consulting, you need to arouse some curiosity about the nature of your call. Yet because you are promoting a competitive service, the client's curiosity will be difficult to arouse. You might begin with:

Consultant: Mr. Todd, my name is Barry Smith. I'm with Value Engineering. The benchmarking results from our design department show that many managers will be pleased with the quality and reliability of our new design simulator. Our clients are saving tens of thousands of dollars.

After you ask for the appointment, you are probably going to get one of a few reactions if you are not granted an appointment initially.

Scenario 1

Mr. Todd: I'm not interested!

Consultant: Mr. Todd, QRST company (mention a competitor company or a company in the client's market) has used our services and is pleased. I would like to share some tangible results (non confidential) enjoyed by them and explain why they have adopted these unique business solutions. What could work for you Mr. Todd, 3:30 today or 9:00 in the morning?

Scenario 2

Mr. Todd: I'm too busy!

Consultant: I know how you feel. Significant dollar savings, Mr. Todd, could make this a priority for you. I am sensitive to people's schedules, and for that reason I use a calendar; I've got mine open here. Would next Tuesday at 8:30 be acceptable or would 10:30 be more convenient?

Scenario 3

Mr. Todd: Tell me about it on the phone!

Consultant: Mr. Todd, a phone presentation of this material would not serve you very well. Using some charts and diagrams in a personal meeting will take 20 minutes and will help give you an accurate view of our approach. Would 3:00 be acceptable, or would 4:30 be better?

Scenario 4

Mr. Todd: Send me some documentation and drawings!

Consultant: Mr. Todd, the documentation that I have requires some personal assistance. However, after our meeting, I will leave hard copy information with you. Would Monday at 9:30 be convenient or would Tuesday at 2:30 be better?

If the receptionist put you through immediately without question, you may be speaking to an intermediate contact. This person will not be the decision maker; however, he or she may be involved in circumstances affecting the final decision.

Whatever the case, treat the person with care. Make your brief presentation and go into your fact-finding questions. Find out a little about the contact's responsibilities at the company. Ask as many questions as you can. Many misconceptions and misunderstandings can exist at first contact. Prejudgments can be made about you and your offering, just as you can jump to conclusions about the client's needs. If a client asks you questions regarding price, you really can't provide an answer. You still won't know enough about what the client is doing with respect to his or her current situation to give accurate answers. But you can generate some positive emotions by stating in general terms your kinds of services and what you are doing for people out in the field. Give the client something. State that you have many services, pricing structures, and alternatives.

At this point, clients often help qualify themselves by asking you a few specific questions, or by making comments regarding their current situation. If a client asks you questions, treat those questions like hot potatoes and ask the same questions as they relate to the client's needs. The quality of the client's answers will tell you how knowledgeable he or she is about your offering. If you know that the real decision maker should have good knowledge of your type of offering and your present contact does not, then you may be talking to the wrong person. Ask yourself, "Am I talking to a decision maker? Can this person give me accurate information?"

If you feel you can do business somewhere within a particular company, then that company qualifies for a visit, regardless of whom you are talking to. If you feel you are talking to the wrong person, ask for another internal name. Try a new approach — another department might be an avenue in reaching an appropriate contact. You only get a portion of your necessary fact-finding for qualification over the phone. This is why the use of the telephone is really your first stage of qualification.

Your goal is to get the appointment with a decision-maker, however, you may have to settle for an intermediate contact. (If your present contact is poor, your personal visit with the person may be the only way to get to the right contact.) Again, give a choice when setting the appointment date. As you close for the appointment say, "For our computer mailing list, your address, please?" Then quickly add, "And your business card title, please?" That title will tell you more about this unknown contact's responsibilities. Then finish your telephone conversation with, "If anyone else should be involved, please ask them to be included in our meeting. Do you think anyone else will attend?" This will help flush out an identity or that others are involved. A non-decision maker may attempt to appear to be the one who makes the decisions. The person may want to appear to his or her superiors as an individual who can come up with new business opportunities. This may be all for the security of the person's present job. Deal with this initial process with patience.

Screening Incoming Calls

Some telephone solicitations will come to you. Some are well-qualified referrals or solid leads from advertising efforts. Yet a subset of these leads will only be looking for information. These can be quite a drain on your time. Qualify them by asking the callers where they got your name. If through a product advertisement, ask how the ad applies to their needs. If they claim they are working on a project involving your services, ask them who else they are evaluating besides your company. Ask them qualifying questions regarding their company. Find out if they are listed in the telephone book. Look at their web site. Run a Dunn & Bradstreet check. Why investigate them so carefully? Again, because some people want information and not your services. This is fine, but you do not have the time.

These people are usually very agreeable and make big promises. Choice questions may smoke out something the client is trying to hide. For example, "Are you going to retrofit one building or the entire plant?" The caller might respond, "Well, it is a small application now, but if it flies we are going to need your services for every plant in the country." Here you have to ask yourself,

"Does this person have enough clout to be making such a claim?" If you sense deception, go with your gut feeling. You might think to yourself, "No way would a busy person waste time for a little free information." Don't kid yourself. The person may be trying to justify a decision already made. If so, in the caller's mind he or she is not wasting time.

The First Appointment

Assume an individual has qualified for an appointment. Now you must prepare for that appointment. Remember, the client has only qualified for the appointment and given you some basic information regarding his or her current situation. Based on implications, use your imagination and prepare other fact-finding questions. Write them down. Along with your prepared approach, bring to the appointment any key information and company marketing tools. When you arrive, carefully look at the facility. How do these people present themselves? Does the company appear to be well managed? Was your appointment kept on time? How does your contact appeal to your senses? All these things help you qualify further.

Qualification requires prioritization when you are involved with several clients. A company you call on may not be under any pressure whatsoever to make a timely decision. Hence as you visit with a client, ask yourself the question, "Am I approaching a company that needs a solution to their problem soon?" In other words, prioritize your opportunities. After all, your time is limited. The old saying, "Go where the money is" has validity. You want to choose clients that use or most readily would use your services.

After your introductions and small talk, open with your presentation. Begin with an introduction to yourself. State that you are there to help the client with his or her goals. Review those goals. Then state, in general, what benefits you offer clients. Present a mission statement and go into some of your company facts or history. If you are in front of a group, have some pre-made transparencies for overhead projection or slides. Review any key topics discussed while you were on the telephone with the client.

The first purpose of your agreement questions is to verify that you have correct information. Ask any new fact-finding questions which can further define the client's situation. Now that you are in front of the client, ask how he or she feels about that situation. Do this by asking what the client likes about it rather than what he or she doesn't like. Ask if the client would like to see any improvements and if so, what kinds of improvements. I hope your fast mind will be discovering client needs you can solve with your services. If so, you can label them as qualified and begin to invest the effort necessary to expose the diagnosed needs to the client. One by one, you want to verify that the customer agrees that what you call a need is indeed a need. This verification of needs is the second purpose of your agreement questions.

Consultant: It sounds like design verification has been a time-consuming and inconvenient task here at Stratum Engineering, right?

Client: Yes, it sure has been.

Consultant: Not only has design verification been a burden for you, the quality has not been of the standard you would like, is that correct?

Client: It's always been a problem.

You want to expose several needs. Cycle through this repetitive process and get more "yes's" for your need discovery.

After you feel that the client understands all of his or her needs, reintroduce one need and a feature of your service that relates to that client need. Now you can exercise the third purpose of your agreement questions: to verify the client's agreement that the benefit of what you can deliver solves the need. Let's look at an example of need and benefit discovery.

Consultant: It sounds like design verification has been a time-consuming and inconvenient task here at Stratum Engineering, right?

Client: Yes, it sure has been.

Consultant: Bob, here is a description and printouts of our own simulation software. Take one. Can you see that using this approach will save you time on the field?

Client: Yes, I suppose so.

Consultant: The extra steps in your project management could be eliminated, couldn't they?

Client: Definitely.

Consultant: And the extra dollar investment would no longer be necessary, true?

Client: Yes.

Consultant: With this approach, you would be able to meet the quality standards you desire, wouldn't you?

Client:: Yes, I would.

All the client's answers, of course, may not have been "yes." (We will discuss other client reactions in Chapter Four.) The point is that by now you should be getting valuable feedback from the client. Continue the introduction of a feature followed by the verification of a related benefit for each need, one by one.

At this point, if indeed you are dealing with an intermediate contact who heavily influences the decision, you will want to find out who approves of the decision from a financial point of view (in other words, who has ultimate veto power). If you ask directly, your dialogue with the intermediate contact may proceed as follows:

Consultant: Who makes the decision, Carl?

Client: Well, I do, Kent.

Consultant: Yes, but who actually signs off on this purchase, Carl, or who financially approves of this purchase?

Client: Oh! That would be Mr. Sorenson.

Technically, your intermediate contact may make the decision from a capability point of view, but you must find out who makes the financial decision.

If the intermediate contact says, "We have it in the budget," inquire whether the budget has been approved or simply submitted for review to the financial decision maker. There is a big and important difference here. By later contacting the financial decision maker, you may discover that this individual needs information to help make the decision or that there are no funds available this year. In a smaller company, the person who makes the decision from a technical point of view and the financial decision maker can be one in the same. In larger companies, however, a small group of people is often involved in the decision. If the latter is the case, you need to know the pecking order. (Chapter Five has more on this subject.)

Demonstration of Capabilities

Notice that in the last example I handed the client a printout from the software and asked him to see the quality. This exemplifies the importance of demonstrations. A demonstration is a great way to introduce features and benefits, and receive valuable feedback from the client.

Suppose your client is well qualified. The client wants to see a simulation. The client wants to prove to him or herself that all those good things about your offering are true. With the information you have gathered on the client's application, you tailor a demonstration for that client's situation. Prepare this in writing; at least, make a detailed outline. Say the same things which exposed those earlier buying emotions during your qualification period. You want, through simulation, to demonstrate the level of your services. Give the client just enough demonstration to stimulate more interest, not an A-Z check-out. Keep it simple. Do not inundate the client with unnecessary information which will create unnecessary objections. There may be an objectionable feature on your services the client would rarely experience in the field. Don't bring it up if it is trivial.

If possible, get the client to come to your office for the demonstration. Unless he or she wants a "coffee break" (a potential situation you should have eliminated by thoroughly qualifying the client), a client's visit shows interest and possible commitment to making a decision. Try to have a colleague help you while you're giving the demonstration. Why? Because often more than one person will attend, and rather than talk to you, the clients may talk among themselves. Much of this talk may be about important applications that you should be aware of. Also, key names of other decision makers may be casually mentioned. If you are busy operating the demonstration, you may miss out on some of this valuable information. If you did not smoke out the real decision maker, he or she may quietly show up for the demonstration and sit off to the side without your knowing that person's identity. Approach the unknown individual and introduce yourself; find out who he or she is. This introduction may be impossible if you are preoccupied with the computer because of a lack of help.

Have your computer set up so your clients do not have to watch you get organized. Work cleanly and efficiently. If you are prepared, demonstrations are great fun. If not, they can be disastrous. Begin with an introduction about you, your company, trends in the industry, and your services. Any lengthy presentation to a client should be done on a day separate from the demonstration day. Do not hand out documents during your demonstrations; you want to keep their eye contact. Present an agenda. Tell them what you are going to do in the demonstration. If you have any visual aids, use them. Begin to reiterate the already discovered needs. Introduce the related features and their benefits as you go along. Tell them what you are doing.

Handle interruptions gracefully. Any time you are interrupted, hear out the client. Then politely state that you will get back to that issue later, and continue with your questioning or explaining. If the client's question is timely, critical, or can be handled quickly, answer it. If you are confronted with a long interruption out of your control, summarize the progress already made and continue.

After you are done, tell the clients what you have done through summarization. Don't shut down and clean up until you are through with the entire meeting. Take mental notes of any newly discovered hot points and write them down. If the right people are indeed present and your needs/benefits discovery went well, you'll want to begin the process of closing at the conclusion of your demonstration. Use any newly discovered information in a benefits summary. Define all the follow-up details and get a strong verbal commitment as to what will follow and when. In the next chapter, we will discuss the process of closing and see how it fits into the total persuasion process.

> *"I hear and I forget, I see and I remember, I do and I understand."*
>
> — CHINESE PROVERB

Summary

1. Always invest in pre-call research to obtain facts about your potential customer's business.

2. Based on your pre-call research, prepare some fact-finding questions before you talk with the client; you want to discover practical needs which can be solved by your offering.

3. Write down all the benefits of your services that can possibly be realized by a given client. You must be able to respond to difficult questions and understand the client's applications.

4. When initially on the telephone, understand that a receptionist's job is to screen unfamiliar calls. Assume a posture of "business as usual" when talking with the receptionist. If you do not already have the name of an internal contact, your initial objective is to get a name of an influential contact inside the company. Realize that you may depend on the receptionist's help. Find out and use the name of the receptionist.

5. When talking with internal contacts, appeal to their company interests and curiosity. Be prepared to overcome any objection to your request for an appointment with a positive perspective contrary to their objections, then offer a choice when setting the appointment time. Ask for the appointment at least a few times.

6. Realize that your internal contact may be an intermediate contact and not a decision maker. Have some questions prepared to help identify his or her role. Find out who that financial decision maker is.

7. If many solicitations come to you, have a good list of qualifying questions for your caller. Don't waste too much time on mere information seekers.

8. Based on mostly technical information, decide whether to invest the time and energy required to prepare for and meet with the client. If you do meet with the client, have additional prepared questions based on your initial contact. Attempt to discover more needs. At this point, you decide whether or not to invest the time and energy necessary to persuade the client to see needs and have the desire to acquire your services.

9. Interruptions can occur many times throughout the persuasion process. They happen fast and explode your train of thought. Handle them tenaciously and get back on track quickly.

10. When with clients, verify their needs one by one. If your offering lends itself to a demonstration, take advantage of this useful selling tool. Try to have the clients come to your facility for the demonstration. Have a colleague assist so your clients talk to you rather than to each other. Introduce the feature of your offering which solves the need and explain the applicable benefit of the feature.

11. Summarize your presentation before packing up to leave. Define all follow-up details and ask for a verbal commitment as to what details will follow and when.

*"Minds are like parachutes: They only
function when open."*

— UNKNOWN

CHAPTER FOUR

Objections, Diversions, and Negotiation

You have been explaining capabilities and benefits to your client; but as I said in the last chapter, the client is not going to say "yes" and accept or understand all the benefits you introduce. Long before you get to the point where you ask for the business, you are going to run into a couple of basic reactions at any time. The two reactions, disinterest and objection, are vague and certainly not agreement responses. For simplicity, I will label them "no" reactions.

If your client is initially disinterested, the individual may not seem to care about increasing his or her business through your offering. (You must be careful not to spend too much time on initially disinterested contacts that continue to be disinterested. If you are selling into the "unaware need," you will run into doubt and disinterest. Again, for this situation, a high degree of selling skill is necessary. Obviously, you would have to see the business potential to continue with this type of client.)

If the client objects, he or she is challenging you for more information. "How is that?" you may ask. When clients object, they are probably thinking of something regarding their situation that might eliminate the feasibility of your offering. Although objections can be expressed as a statement, often they are in question form. You might hear comments like, "What about this?" and "What about that?" In a sense, the client is qualifying you; the client is actively involved. This is an indication that the client may consider making a buying decision.

The client's objection may be an indirect inquiry about how your services will work in the many special situations the client may occasionally encounter on the job. During your qualification stage, you learned of the client's business or way of doing things; but not every special situation, some of which may be vitally important to the client. And, yes, the client will either forget or not bother to mention these special situations in the early stages of your qualification. Initially, clients want to know if your offering can handle the basics of their needs. Hence other critical information will dribble out later in the consultation process in the form of objections. Avoid letting this frustrate you; it is fruitless to cloud your mind with questions like "Why didn't he or she mention that earlier?" And, of course, never challenge the client verbally with this question. Understand this phenomenon and patiently deal with it.

Some objections are based on the client's misunderstandings. You may have received agreements earlier on specific points the person now questions you about. Why? Because the client simply may have thought you were talking about something else or not have given you his or her full attention. Misunderstandings are common. In this type of situation, don't tell the client he or she is wrong. It is unnecessary to scold the client with "as I mentioned earlier ..." Ask more questions to uncover their perceptions. Accept these things through understanding and be happy that you are getting the feedback that you need.

How to Handle the Objection

How do you handle an objection? First, listen to the client until he or she is finished. People do not want to be interrupted, no matter how excited you are about the information you are about to give them. Wait a moment or two after they offer an objection. Give them a chance to clarify their objection or say it in different terms, then question their objection:

Client:	I still don't think your capabilities will do.
Consultant:	They won't?
Client:	No. I don't think your design approach will allow us to move our projects along any faster.

Clients may realize their confusion as they restate and answer the objection. The client could have quickly followed the last comment above with, "Wait a minute. I can have you inhouse during construction and installation, right?" If a client does not restate or answer the objection, you state, "If I understand you correctly, ..." and finish your sentence with an accurate translation of the objection you can solve:

Client:	You consultants are all alike. You're not available when we need you!
Consultant:	If I understand you correctly, Joe, what you want is solid value and support, isn't that right?
Client:	Yes, you are darned right.
Consultant:	Then let's discuss what you want out of me in addition to the programs I offer as standard. We might then use that agreement as a foundation for us to continue negotiation, is that fair enough?

Remember to end your statement with words which solicit the client's agreement when verifying your translation and solution of the objection. By agreeing, the client indirectly tells you, "OK, I now understand the benefits that solve the problems expressed through my objection." In this example, the benefits were the service/support practices.

If the client has a legitimate objection which is related to shortcomings of your offering, answer it. If the client knows the answer to an objection related to a shortcoming of your offering, he or she is testing your credibility. Regardless, provide an honest answer. If you are indeed being tested, you gain that credibility. Besides, if the client knows the answer already, your response won't be a shock. If the shortcoming can be minimized, do so to reduce disappointment. Minimize it by comparing that particular shortcoming as a minute concern with respect to the benefits the client really wants. Do this by letting the client tell you what the important benefits are through your use of questions. In this example, we finish with a fact-finding question that offers a choice which makes a comparison of benefits:

Client:	Your bid is absurd!
Consultant:	How is that?
Client:	Well, the price just seems to be a little out of line.
Consultant:	We know you like the services, right?
Client:	Very much so, yes.
Consultant:	Remember that support program we took care to outline for your unique concerns, Mr. Smith?
Client:	Yes.
Consultant:	Weren't you pleased with that program?

Client:	Yes.
Consultant:	Then don't you think that the little extra investment in the short term will more than offset the hard cost and dull headaches you will experience with a poor support program that could trouble you for the entire life of the project?
Client:	Well ... uh ... yes.
Consultant:	I think so, too.

Get back to what is important and minimize the unimportant. If you receive a huge objection that prevents business, then your qualifying process did not identify it earlier. Sometimes it cannot be helped. Again, you are doing the best job you can in a limited amount of time.

Often an objection is the client's reluctance to accept something different. Your services may appear different. The client may have to operate differently. The client may have to do paperwork in a different manner to accommodate your services. Listen to the client. Ask the client his or her objection in question form. Get the client to elaborate on it. Find out what is really important to the client. Then minimize any differences by introducing critical benefits needed by the client. Slowly get the client to accept new ideas through the offering of benefits he or she is really seeking. Make sure you get their agreement as to the elimination of their objection before you proceed.

Time to Start Closing

By now you should be receiving some positive feedback from the client. Remember when we talked about the consultant making decisions for the client? You did it while discovering the client's needs with respect to your offering. These were needs the client might not have realized he or she had. Hence you made decisions ahead of the client; you decided he or she was qualified for business. Remember that? Then you shifted gears from a decision-making mode to a consulting mode to bring them up to speed with knowledge. You did this by exposing the benefits of your services that solved needs. You received verification of the client's positive reactions to your offering by getting agreements. You offered proof and gave demonstrations. You established buying emotions. You overcame objections through interpretation, followed by clarification. But your decision-making muscles had relaxed and your consulting muscles had flexed during this period. So how long do you go on consulting and problem solving? You have to decide for the client that he or she is ready for a decision. Because you have to switch gears again and put the brakes on a lot of consulting momentum, it's easy to forget to flex those decision-making muscles and not ask for the decision.

Begin efforts toward asking for the decision with an assumptive attitude. You assume the client will proceed because you know that your services truly offer value for the client and because you have done a good job with getting agreement to the benefits of your offering. Yet the client may still resist you. "Why on earth would he or she still remain reluctant?" you may think to yourself. Because all this new information hasn't totally settled in the client's mind, and because he or she is not yet feeling completely secure about the change involved. But you and the client, practically speaking, cannot wait for these things to happen. You cannot wait because the client truly has enough information and any additional information would slow the person down. Remember, making good business decisions in a time-efficient manner is what we get paid for. If you wait too long before asking for the decision, the client will forget some of the information required for the decision. The decision-making phenomenon follows an efficiency curve, and the best time to begin the closing sequence is at its peak. If you are worried about the client having enough facts or "emotional comfort" for making a decision, remember that new facts and changing emotions will occur in the client's mind throughout the life of the project.

Trial Close

To help the person through this difficult time of decision-making, begin the closing process by applying what I call constructive pressure. When and how do you do this? First of all, don't "suddenly" ask for the client's business; instead, use a "closing sequence." Begin this sequence during the handling of objections. The client will first throw out some primary objections during your introduction of benefits to check your credibility and qualification status. Answer a few of these. You will gain credibility and receive positive feedback from the client. After these few initial objections, begin the closing sequence by applying constructive pressure through the use of a trial close. Trial closes imply ownership and commitment. They consist of fact-finding questions which offer a choice and test the positive buying emotions of the client. If the client responds positively to your trial close, he or she is indeed ready to accept your offering. Remember our last example when talking about objections. You could very well add a trial close onto that dialogue, as in the following two examples:

1. "Would a monthly or a semi-annual installment be better for you?"

2. "By the way, Mr. Client, which construction installation date are you looking at? Is it the first or the middle of the month?"

Figure 4.1: Negotiation Flow Chart

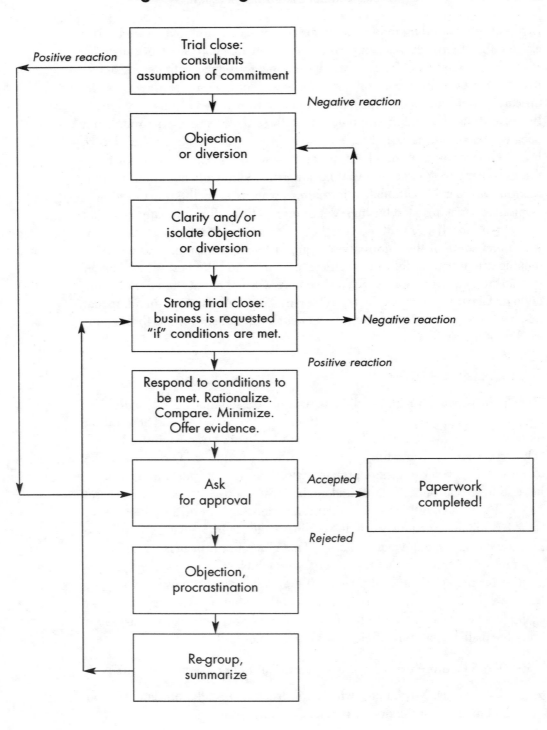

Begin to imply ownership by relating to events that will occur after the client takes ownership. The client may respond, "I'm not ready for that yet." You respond, "Fine, but there is a reason for my asking: I plan my schedules with my staff. I try to keep a close relationship with them so they will respond to any new customer demands. Is this acceptable to you?" What you did here was take the client off the hook and let the client know that he or she could count on you for service. Take a look at the upper part of Figure 4.1: Negotiation Flow Chart. Notice that I invoked a trial close, as indicated by the top box in the flow chart, and received the objection (next box), "I'm not ready for that yet." I then clarified the objection with an explanation that eliminated the objection.

The Diversion

After you overcome the client's initial objections and after a simple trial close or two, you will begin to identify the more major objections. As you respond to the more major objections, you may notice a change in the client's pace — either the pace may suddenly pick up or an already strong pace may begin to drop off. If the pace picks up, you will experience interruptions and diversions from the client. Why? Because the client might be wrestling with the decision and is thinking of a million things at once. We've discussed interruptions in the last chapter, but what is a diversion? A diversion is when a person responds to a statement you made with a response that is unrelated to your statement. In most cases, you will experience a diversion with the client offering an agreement or positive statement which you as a consultant have solicited, but which is quickly followed with an unrelated statement about another issue. For example:

Consultant: It's our design procedure that is going to simplify your tasks, true?

Client: Yeah. Can we license your software?

In this example, the client half heard you and gave you a weak agreement to shut you up in order to say what was on his or her mind. This type of diversion is not intentional. Again, the client is thinking of many things and has many things to say. At this point, you don't know if your design procedure is important to the client, nor do you know if licensing software is critical. Many consultants relax when they hear that positive statement or agreement which they requested; however, if that agreement is minimized by an unrelated statement, then you as a listener have to seriously question the quality of that initial agreement. Therefore if you have been talking about a particular feature of your offering for a while and suddenly you are diverted, you'll have to quickly (but politely) get back on track again and ask if that particular part of your services was indeed important to the client.

If it turns out that your design standard practice is not critical, you might discover that you have an experienced negotiator who only wants cut-rate services. This is something very important for you to know because it will determine your action; you may not be able to help the client out in that case. If you are dealing with an experienced negotiator, know that the diversions you encounter may very well be intentional. Another example:

Consultant: Can I get my people back at the office rolling on this today?

Client: (smiling and nodding "yes") Can we use your software for this small side project that we have?

(Get back on track with your need to get a solid agreement.)

Consultant: Based on what we've already talked about, Mr. Client, can I get my people rolling on the main project? (View the second and third boxes in Figure 4.1: Negotiation Flow Chart.) The consultant received a diversion and then isolated that diversionary comment made by the client.)

At this point, when the pace is fast and you're near a business agreement, it is tempting to answer the client's random or bargaining questions (diversions). After all, you want the business. But resist temptation. If you are tenacious, gentle, and firm with diversions, you can maintain control of the negotiation, get your questions answered, and attain your business objective. As you maintain control, the client may drop a bargaining issue or even forget about it. If the client diverts to the same issue two and three times, then understand it as something the client really wants you to respond to. Now it might be time for a strong trial close.

Strong Trial Close

If the client does indeed challenge you on a service or construction date, offer a "strong trial close." A strong trial close requests the business "if" you can meet certain requirements set up by the client. Hence your reply to such a challenge might be, "If I can guarantee this construction date (or extra service), can you approve your paperwork today?" If you are now greeted with silence, put a zipper on it and keep quiet. Wait for the client to go ahead. Don't let the pressure of that dead silence work on you. It's for the client. Relax and let it work on him or her. If an extremely long pause occurs, break the client's paralysis. (View the fourth box in Figure 4.1: Negotiation Flow Chart.)

Consultant:	Let's go ahead with your decision today. (Hand the client the contract if there is one.)

If at all possible, have your contract with you. This act is a closing tool in itself. As you bring out the contract, prepare to make changes if necessary. By having the contract completed, you can capitalize on a positive buying climate after a strong trial close. In other words, you can ask for the business and process the paperwork right on the spot. There may be highly competitive situations when you can lose a client just because you didn't have your paperwork with you and your competition later showed up with theirs before you had a chance to return with your contract!

Regrouping to Close Again

Let's say you finish a closing sequence and ask for the business; but instead of silence, you get procrastination in the form of "I want to think it over." Realize that you did not get a "yes" decision. Whenever a closing sequence does not bring a "yes" decision, follow it with another closing sequence. Although your first closing sequence did not get a "yes," emotionally it is still working on the client. The client feels that constructive pressure. But you have more work to do. To get to the next sequence, you have to "regroup." (Take a look at the last three boxes of the Negotiation Flow Chart, Figure 4.1.) To regroup, let the client off the hook with an empathetic statement supporting the client's need to review the issue. This eases the pressure. Then begin another closing sequence by summarizing progress already made, one point at a time. Verify all points and check their validity so you can find out what's holding up the client.

Client:	I want to think it over.
Consultant:	Of course. I suppose you want all this information to settle a bit.
Client:	Yes.
Consultant:	And will you give it very careful review?
Client:	Of course.
Consultant:	So that I can leave with some clarity, what is it you wanted to think most critically about? Was it the ease of implementation of the design procedure?
Client:	No, that seems fine.
Consultant:	Was it the speed of the design simulation?

> Client: No.
>
> Consultant: Was it the quality you were worried about?
>
> Client: Oh, gosh no.

If you feel good about things, then stop and let the client sleep on it. But if you feel something is not quite right, go through each point, one by one. Was it this? Was it that? Every time the client responds "no" to the assumption of possible problems, he or she is guided to a "yes" decision through a process of elimination. Additionally, the need for more offerings may be discovered. Furthermore, it is difficult to price your offering until it is defined. (I hope by now you realize you are with a client who wants value, and not a cut-rate bargain.) Price will have to be compared to your unique benefits when tough competition is present. If forced to compare "apples to apples," then your pricing should reflect such a comparison to be competitive.

If before you get to mentioning price the client picks out a couple of points and objects to them, go back to a strong trial close. Begin with a reassuring statement like, "In the pursuit of your goals, if you could convince yourself that I could solve these problems with a solid plan, would you be ready to do business today?" If the response is "yes," get the client to agree to your approach to solving the problems with your questioning skills. If the response is "no," find out what the deterrent is. After the client answers his or her own objections, say, "Mr. Client, you are going to be pleased with having us on your team. Let's do what makes sense and go ahead today." Hand over the contract and wait. If you do not get a "yes" decision, ask if the bid price is the problem. Regardless of who brings up the price objection, ask, "How much in excess do you think the bid is?" After you get that figure, get the client to compare that amount to the extra benefits he or she would be receiving. You may have to add or subtract services to reach a strike price.

Whatever the objection, make comparisons whenever the benefits are not obvious to the client. If the client mentions a shortcoming of your offering and follows that comment with the word "but," then continues with positive comments regarding your offering, offer a close based on those positive comments:

> Client: This design project is awfully radical, but that design simulation is the best I've ever seen.
>
> Consultant: Yes, it is. And it's that capability that is going to simplify your tasks. Let's fill out some paperwork and get going.

If the client mentions something positive about your offering and follows that comment with the word "but," then continues with a negative comment regarding your offering, use a strong trial close on that negative comment:

Client:	This design simulation is the best thing I've ever seen, but that software looks difficult to use.
Consultant:	If I can offer training, can we go ahead today?

Let's say you have been using sequence after sequence and nicely regroup between each one, without a "yes" decision. If all seems hopeless, pack up some materials as if to conclude the meeting. Then say, "Well, Mr. or Ms. Client, I feel that I have not served you well. We did agree that you are looking for a solution. Could you help me with any comments so that I could be more of an asset to you?" With this question, you might discover an issue that you absolutely never would have expected. You may then have one last opportunity for the business.

One thing the flow chart does not indicate is how to deal with different personalities. As a buyer, or when the client is in a buying mode, the client will display a personality orientation. This will become clear by the types of objections that are raised. The more you are aware of the client's buyer orientation, the more you can appeal to his or her reality. For instance, it's important that you let doubtful clients feel they have some breathing room. Offer an escape route out of the deal in case their doubts are later validated. Be relaxed yet firm with the control clients. Let them tell you how the world turns and don't argue. But when you are pushed for unnecessary information, be firm and stay on track. Ask questions. Let them convince themselves. Use more questions to discover their past practices and/or experiences which make them feel so strongly. Ask them to consider another perspective. Always ask for their agreement. If they staunchly refuse to answer a clearly understandable question (using diversionary tactics), realize they are refusing to answer. Let it go. If their answer is not conditional for your progress, move on to another topic. For clients who procrastinate, make comparisons and analogies with common examples to minimize worries. A procrastinating client usually makes decisions only when the need is pressing, almost to the point of being too late. Be patient, yet keep an eye on your progress and time management. You may want to put this type of client on the back burner as a priority. For individuals with glaring egos, compare what they do with the highest industry standards. If prospects are offensive, keep cool and don't "react" to their negativity. Try to soften the situation. If unsuccessful, leave and try another day when the "climate" is better.

People want to be right, listened to and understood. You, as the consultant, have to somewhat deny yourself what we all crave — ego satisfaction — when dealing with challenging clients. If you feed your own ego, clients will shy away from you and your income will be adversely affected. Make the client feel that you care. Clients have to like you, trust you, and respect you.

> *"If you refuse to settle for anything less than the best, that's what it will give you."*
>
> — W. SOMERSET MAUGHAM

Summary

1. An objection is the client's way of saying, "I need more information; I don't understand yet." Therefore an objection is an opportunity for you to have more involvement with the client.

2. An objection can also be based on a misunderstanding. Respond by restating the objection to the client in question form. This will give the client a chance to clarify or elaborate on the objection.

3. Minimize any legitimate shortcomings of your offering by comparing it to what is truly important to the client. Do this in question form.

4. Objections can also be based on the client's reluctance to accept something that is different. Be patient. Involving the client in a demonstration can minimize his or her negative feelings.

5. Once an objection is overcome, ask for the client's agreement to verify that there no longer is a problem.

6. After you handle a few primary objections, which establishes your credibility, do a trial close. This is the point where you stop consulting the client and assume his or her commitment to a "yes" decision. Ask a question about events which would follow after the client owns your services. In other words, you imply ownership.

7. As you handle the more critical objections, the pace will pick up. Be gentle and firm when you handle diversions; maintain control of the flow of information and/or negotiation. Offer a strong trial close that requests ownership if certain conditions (which will eliminate the critical objection or challenge) are met.

8. If you ask for the client's approval and you receive an objection or procrastination, regroup and summarize the progress made. Verify your summarization, remove any existing barriers and ask for the decision.

9. All clients will require the basic questioning process, but some clients' buyer-personality types will require that you ask more questions (and take more time) than others. Many clients will require direct evidence or analogies/examples through comparisons of various kinds.

*"When you're through changing,
you're through."*

— BRUCE BARTON

CHAPTER FIVE

Account Strategy, Proposals, and Contracts

Approaching an account for the first time is like approaching a black box. You do some research, which will give you useful information; yet it has a history, much of which is not documented. The company probably has an organizational chart indicating who reports to whom and, within larger organization, which groups support various activities. But the chart may be quite different from how the company actually functions. "Functional charts" are rarely verbalized or written down. They are formed by the strengths of the company's employees and internal relationships. These employees and their "functions," in concert with the actual organizational chart, influence how information is processed and thus how decision makers select solutions. As you become familiar with an account, having a strategy to deal with company history, organization, key players, relationships, and competition will maximize your chances for success.

Cracking the New Large Account

An experience of mine provides a classic example of the importance of defining a new large account. (This is really an example of learning from a mistake.) I was calling on a large government contractor. I'd been in contact with a group of engineers for roughly six months as their project unfolded. I had worked hard developing these contacts and consulting with them on application problems through my offering. I assumed that Engineering had the total power to make the decision. Suddenly, unknown to me, paperwork for new services was released from Engineering to a Contracts person and then to Procurement. All this occurred within three weeks. I had no idea such a decision-making process was going to take place; nor did I know what roles these last two individuals played in the process. Fortunately, I got the new business. As a matter of fact, the procurement agent had phoned the order into my office. Because I hadn't anticipated these events, I wasn't even in touch with these people during this critical time. To this day, I can only guess why I got the business. I think it was because none of the competition had followed up with the last two contacts either. Hurting for information, Procurement went back to Contracts and Contracts went back to Engineering for some advice. Because I had worked hard with Engineering, the advice given out was in my favor. However, if the competition had followed up with everyone involved in the decision-making process and had spent less effort with Engineering, they might have received the business instead of me. When I found out that Procurement had called my office with the contract award, I was both relieved and privately embarrassed — relieved because everyone said "Good job," and embarrassed because I didn't even see it coming.

I quickly called Procurement to find out how the decision-making process evolved. I didn't want to make the same mistake twice. Briefly, the decision process went like this: Engineering has to come up with a few contractor choices based on their needs. The Contracts person acts as an unbiased buffer between Engineering and Procurement. Contracts says it can't push paperwork through until Engineering gets more than one possible contractor. The theory here is to limit Engineering from choosing too much consulting. Therefore the Contracts person simply looks at meeting specifications, not exceeding them.

A legitimate Engineering complaint regarding this process is that Contracts may not take all issues into consideration. Mere specifications often do not reflect these issues. Once paperwork is released to Contracts, the consultant is not supposed to contact the contract officers in that department. This is to ensure unbiased decision making. Hence the consultant is supposed to anticipate the release of paperwork and contact the Contracts person before that release. At that time, you can work with the Contracts person on the non-specifications aspects of your offering. You, as the consultant, provide the very necessary communication between these people which they are prohibited from carrying on. Once the paperwork leaves Contracts, Procurement chooses among the contractor choices closest in bid price. By meeting with the Procurement contact early in the game, you might extol the details of your bid. If you learn of the decision process, plan your strategy, and reach the key players in the decision process with pre-planned meetings, you know you have done your job. You would also have a solid feeling for an award and not a vague feeling of possible success.

According to their process, these contacts shouldn't have gone back to their preceding contact for information; however, no consultant was there to help them out. Because they had gone by the book before and received tremendous heat from big buying mistakes, going back to their contacts for decision-making aid at the risk of getting into trouble was an easy option. At some large facilities, I was shocked to find procurement individuals with little or no technical background. Again, here is where the consultant's input is critical. If you help people make decisions they want to make, they will want to give you the business.

When approaching larger organizations, obtain an annual report and, if possible, an organizational chart. Seek out their web site. If your services warrant an initial high-level contact, begin with a top-down approach. You may need the executive to sign off on his or her company's investigation into your offering. Alternatively, the executive may direct you to middle management. If a company's middle management is currently "looking" for new services and you have not yet contacted an executive, a quick and brief check with upper management is wise. The V.P., owner, or CEO may say to you, "We are indeed looking, funds are approved and my people will decide. Thanks for calling!" Hence you work with middle management. When involved in selling to more than one person or a group of people who have input which affect the final decision, plan your approach. Write down all their names, titles, roles, potential problems or road blocks, and the possible actions to be taken with each person to help improve your position. If, in the end, this group of middle managers states they are going with your competition's offering and you feel strongly that they are making a mistake, then going over their heads to the top can be a valid tactic. You may very well rock the boat a bit, don't use this approach as a matter of course. Use it only when you feel you have a chance of turning that decision into a good one (the award of your services).

A word of caution about situations where more than one decision maker is involved, whether in the private or public sectors: You will run into people who will intentionally try to point you in the wrong direction. They will use the sheer size of their organization to send you on time-consuming wild goose chases. They may not like your offering or have some special interest in mind. Remember that as you talk to one person, that's only one source of information. Don't let one person discourage you. Just keep doing your detective work until you receive information which agrees with other information. If you discover that a "wild-goose-chase contact" is one of the decision makers, you then must make a plan to handle the situation. This is another kind of strategy involving emotions. As you set up meetings, you do not want to create a situation where you leave the "goose" out of the picture. Nor do you want to put him or her in the position of bad-mouthing you to the other decision makers before you have a chance to develop these relationships. Set preliminary appointments and sell your good contacts first. Quickly follow with an appointment with the "goose"; this way he or she will not feel left out. Tell the goose who you have seen. If you have been successful with the others, let subtle peer pressure work to quiet down the individual. You want that person fighting you as little as possible. Yes, many times you will be in a meeting and everything is going great—except there will be that one person present who you wish would take a "permanent coffee break." If that person is a powerful decision maker, just stay with him or her and work to change things around.

Competitive Situations

Let's define a competitive situation as one where there is more than one consultant working to a new client. When faced with this circumstance, fully realize that your position may be no better than that of the other consultant. As a matter of fact, you may as well assume that you are the underdog. After all, you do not know much about the existing relationships between the other consultants and the client. With this sensitive awareness, I hope you will leave no stone unturned. Talk to all the players involved in the decision process. Of course, you want to do the basics better than the competition. You need to find out what the client is trying to accomplish. What does the client want?

Timing can be critical in competitive situations. Initially, clients may be shopping around. They will be in a learning mode and you are part of their survey for information. Clients want to find out what is available in an attempt to solve their need. Therefore in this situation, do not come in with a really strong effort during the beginning of their search, but do plant a few seeds in their mind. If you do go in with a strong effort during the early phase of the client's investigations, your good information will get cold by the time anybody is ready to make a decision.

After the client has had a chance to meet with the competition, you know the client is prepared for you. Now the client should have many intelligent and relevant questions for you. By the types of questions the client might ask, you will know that he or she has been talking to the competition. Treat these questions like "hot potatoes" and isolate what is important to the client. You might ask, "What are the other consultants doing that you like?" If the client brings up a benefit you can easily provide, you might respond, "Ah, yes. We used to do it that way, but we've improved on that by taking it a step further. After extensive customer contact, here is what we've done," and make the introduction to your benefit. If the client brings up something negative with respect to the competition, reinforce the emotion. Feed it back to the client with, "Yes, Ms. Jones, I hear that all the time; it really is a problem, isn't it?" If the client does not bring up anything negative about the competition and you know of some negative aspects of the competition's offering, you bring them up. Do it tactfully by asking the client about the details offered by the competition which are negative.

Consultant:	Did you notice how old their software is?
Client:	Yes, I did.
Consultant:	Did you check to see if it had all the design modules that we can offer?
Client:	No, I didn't.
Consultant:	You might want to investigate that a little more closely. Any savings realized from their services would soon be overshadowed by the turn-around time and accuracy of our services. Can you see that possibility?
Client:	I sure can!

On the other hand, the competition might be saying negative things about your company or services.

Client:	I hear you are going out of business.
Consultant:	Where did you hear that?
Client:	From somebody.
Consultant:	(slight laugh) I can't believe it. I've heard that tactic before. And frankly, can you see where that can get old, fast? Tell me, Mr. Client, did they say our engineering is done by high school summer help, too?
Client:	Yes, as a matter of fact, they did.
Consultant:	Well, of course, neither is accurate. Do you see the awkward position the competition has put you in? They instilled a

question in your mind with respect to our credibility. And on top of that, you had to go through the awkward task of confronting me with it. I think you have to ask yourself, "What else are they telling me that's not true?" (Pause) Is that the kind of company you want to do business with?

Know what your competitors are doing and scrutinize their strengths and weaknesses. Understand their services well enough to set yourself apart with a unique approach and offering. Strong familiarity with your competition will come in handy because you will never know when you will be invited into a competitive situation without prior knowledge that an opportunity even exists. There you'll be, sitting in a meeting with several people involved in the decision. The competition has already been through initial and possibly final consultations. You have little information and you have not established any relationships. These situations happen and they are tough, but they are not impossible to overcome. At this point, if there is some time before a decision has to be made, avoid giving out too much information before you know their issues and concerns. Ask, "What is the problem with the solution you are strongly considering?" If you get a reply of, "Nothing is wrong," ask, "Is there something missing that you would like to see?" (Again, be aware of the possibility that you may be "used" to justify a decision that's already been made.) If you have been invited into a real opportunity, ask several questions. During the meeting, take note of the body language to learn the pecking order. Identify the financial decision maker, as well as all the other players involved in the decision. If you have time before they award a contract, get back to them with a planned strategy and presentation. If you don't have time, you are going to have to do your best right then and there in that initial meeting.

Going Out on a Limb

An effective support system of your organization will give you the confidence to go "out on a limb." Let's suppose the client wants something very special and you don't know that you can meet his or her needs. Chances are you can't, but you're not sure. At this point you say nothing negative. As a matter of fact, you state that you may be able to do it. What you have done here is given yourself the opportunity to go home and have a meeting about the situation. Furthermore, you are still the good guy in the eyes of the client who is taking ownership of your services. That feeling is working on the client overnight, so if you come back with an alternative that is acceptable but not exactly what the client wants, you have a good chance at the business. And if you can't do anything for the client, you can promptly come back and tell the client.

New Business from Existing Accounts

Your established customer base is a source of more business. Changes in their business or growth will create a requirement for more of your offering. Maintain communication with them. Even if they are well serviced and satisfied, you want to let them know that you are available. Make it easy for them to contact you if they reach out for information. Become familiar with as many pertinent contacts within a company as you can. What one person might not think to say (or won't say) regarding their company's future plans, the other will. Know their titles, responsibilities, and implicit concerns regarding their business and how it relates to your offering. If they are in engineering, meeting specifications will be a concern. With the project manager, return on investment may be the concern. With the CEO or president, overall impact on the company's goals will be the concern. You should be on top of things enough to anticipate any changes the client may be involved in.

At times no matter how much fact finding and customer communication you do, you just won't see some changes coming. Your own customer will hit you with a surprise. It is possible a customer will have a new project going and not tell you about it because he or she assumes that your company's capabilities can't meet the new project's needs. That's why you should share with your customers any new non-confidential information as soon as you learn of it. Keep all of your promises and follow up. If it is not obvious by now, know that a consultant is also part detective.

How and When to Use Lunch

Lunch is something you can use very effectively, during good and bad situations. First of all, it gets customers away from the work environment. They may then share information with you that they would not share at their place of business. But lunch is something you do not want to use carelessly. If you offer lunch frequently and needlessly, clients may expect a lunch every time you see them. Furthermore, if lunch becomes regular and routine, key information may no longer come your way. My point is that you want lunch to work for you and not against you.

If you do decide to offer lunch, your timing is important. If after much work you find yourself beginning to win over a new client, then take him or her out to lunch. Let the lunch augment your already positive momentum. But never expect a lunch in itself to win over a client. If a client becomes a new customer, you may want to go out to lunch. Alternatively, you may want to wait until business is concluded before going to lunch. Again, your timing is important. Use your own judgment. If things are going well with a long-established client, offer lunch in a random fashion. Be a little unpredictable with your invitations. Give your current customers a chance to appreciate the lunch in exchange for your appreciation for their business. An exception to all this is if you are involved in a traditional "relationship sell" where entertainment may very well be an expected industry standard.

Client Strategy Profile

During your account development efforts, take some time, somewhere quiet with a cup of coffee or tea, and make notes on the following:

1. Client company history and current goals.

2. Client growth status; up, down, or stagnant.

3. Buying history for your or similar offerings.

4. Players involved in decision; names, titles, and to whom they report.

5. Functional operation of client company.

6. How will using your services affect the players involved in the decision positively and negatively?

7. What is the quality of your relationship with these players and decision makers? Do you come as a warm referral or as a stranger? Is there any name recognition?

8. How does any change in personnel or someone "new to the job" affect your position positively or negatively?

9. What is your position vs. competition?

10. What is their perception of your offering?

11. Can you create "compelling" reasons why the client company would use your offering?

12. How does this opportunity compare to others you have in the pipeline?

13. What questions have you developed to uncover their perceptions, problems, and goals?

14. What action activities with calendar deadlines can you assign to these numbered items to remove any obstacles and position yourself positively?

Field Implementation Plan and Forecast

It is important to maintain a simple implementation plan for field activities. This is an outline of objectives and tactics, with time frames for the execution of those tactics. Each objective would have a corresponding tactic for implementation. The following is a simplified example of such a plan.

How will the $X million goal be generated?

1. **Objective:** Maximize repeat/follow-on business and referrals from established customers.

   Tactic: Generate current customer list. Stay with once per quarter.

2. **Objective:** Leverage vendor relations.

   Tactic: Introduce yourself to their salespeople. Inform them of your business profile. Meet for lunch once per quarter.

3. **Objective:** New business from new programs.

   Tactic: List and profile named accounts. Pursue and qualify bids. Make two new business calls per week. Get referrals. Write down interim objectives for each profiled account.

4. **Objective:** Develop outer geographical area.

   Tactic: Call and line up a trip once per quarter. See multiple companies.

5. **Objective:** Leverage business partners.

   Tactic: Visit with them whenever possible. Make phone contact on a monthly basis. Advocate mutual customer support.

6. **Objective:** Attain quarterly $ goal for current and future years.

   Tactic: After a culmination of the above activities, net out a prospect list, each with a dollar forecast. Is your prospect list long enough for $ goal attainment? Track year-to-date progress.

I've mentioned a forecast for new business. Forecasting helps you prioritize time spent on accounts. How does one forecast? There is no exact way to forecast business. Some professionals use a spread sheet and typically will list the company project name, dollar amount, time frame, and a number representing the probability of winning business. This number can depend on many factors. For example:

1. Is your potential client technically qualified?
2. Are your services in contention with existing competition?
3. Are your services highly favored for selection?
4. Are your services being exclusively selected, with all competition eliminated?
5. Have all issues been discussed with a decision maker or a non-decision maker?
6. Has a proposal format been submitted to a decision maker?
7. Has that decision maker responded to your proposal?
8. Have final papers been submitted?
9. Have papers actually been signed off?
10. Is there funding? If not, what are the chances of the project being funded and in what time frame?

These factors, in conjunction with any historical trends in your business, will help you come up with a forecast probability number. Obviously, all forecasts can be as detailed as you wish to make them. Yet they provide a revenue projection, thus helping you to define and focus priorities.

Proposals, Bids, and Contracts

When presenting a proposal to a client, it should be integrated with standard legal provisions, terms, and conditions. There are many boilerplate legal contracts in print, from which you can cut and paste or modify clauses to customize your own contract. If the contractual relationship is complex, do not hesitate to retain the services of an attorney. Here are some clauses that may be a part of a contract proposal submitted by a contractor to a client for simple and straightforward services (the "aware need").

Project Scope

This proposal for the complete preparation and painting of an office building located at _____ Bird Avenue of Anywhere, California. It is a two-story, 3500 square foot home with 14 windows and three doors, which includes front and rear entries. It is a wooden-sided structure approximately 70 years of age. Existing landscape will pose no problems. Everybody affected by the work in progress will be notified in writing.

Responsibility

_____ will act as prime contractor and will manage this job in its entirety until its agreed-upon completion date of ____/____/____. Small changes with schedule or procedure, if easily implemented by either party, can be worked out by both parties to this contract in good faith. Any major adjustments affecting time, labor, and materials must be put in writing and may result in extra charges over and above this proposal. The goal is to complete this project within the guidelines of this proposal to the satisfaction of the client.

Termination

Either party may terminate this agreement at any time upon written notice from either party, based on a breach of contract or an inability of either party to comply with any obligation pursuant to this agreement. Costs incurred by either party, up to the termination date, may result in a cost settlement or reimbursement, depending on an itemized "deliverable" work-in-progress. Any damages may result in litigation.

Time and Materials

1. Pressure wash loose paint, five hours per side.
2. Hand scrape old paint, five hours per side.
3. Patch woodwork if needed, five hours per side.
4. Sand the patch work, three hours per side.
5. Touch up window glazing. Rack and putty, five hours per side.
6. Prime walls and windows with 123 interior/exterior water-base primer sealer (one coat), six hours per side.
7. Brush base color with semi-gloss, water-base paint (two coats), 12 hours per side.

8. Brush trim color with semi-gloss, water-base paint (two coats), eight hours per side.

9. Paint exit door with semi-gloss, water-base paint (two coats), four hours per side.

Cost

Labor time = 212 hours	$XXX.XX
Materials (paint, primer, miscellaneous materials)	<u>YYY.YY</u>
Total	$ZZZ.ZZ

Payments

Fifty percent down upon signing of contract, with balance due at job's completion. Payment can be made by personal check, cash, or money order.

(End your contract with a signature block.)

It is nice to have the opportunity to submit your own contract; however, you may find yourself submitting a proposal to a sealed-bid solicitation, open to many of your competitors. Avoid signing any contract you do not feel comfortable with or engaging with any client who you feel is not credible. Here are some clauses that may be presented to you by the client.

To secure sealed bids for the supply of _____ services.

1. Bidders shall state, as part of their bid proposal, a definite completion date for the entire work.

2. Previous experience to supply _____ design will be taken into consideration when awarding this bid.

3. Each bidder is to bid a complete work in accordance with specifications herein. Partial bid portions of the work will not be acceptable.

4. A complete set of drawings and documentation shall be supplied as part of the bid proposal. Equipment furnished by the successful bidder as part of the service delivered shall be warranted for a minimum period of ____ year (s) from the date of acceptance. This warranty shall be included with the bid proposal.

5. Any costs incurred by the supplier due to warranty requirements are to be included as part of the equipment costs.

6. The successful bidder shall agree to defend, at his or her own expense, any and all suits alleging patent infringement by use or release of any equipment supplied.

7. Installation of all equipment shall be included in the bid price. All hardware, etc., required for installation of the equipment shall be furnished by the bidder.

8. Comprehensive instruction and maintenance manuals shall be provided for all equipment. The manuals shall provide sufficient and concise information, including schematics, operational procedures, and a parts list, to permit quick and efficient maintenance and repair of the equipment by a competent maintenance technician.

9. Manufacturers' brochures of all equipment listed on the bid form shall be included as part of the bid.

Setting competitive price levels for your services must yield an acceptable profit margin. Your price levels may depend, in part, on historical or established market conditions, how many clients you can service per unit of time, and your costs plus overhead.

Cost Justification

Suppose you are offering a service involving the aforementioned "unaware need." A written cost justification can be used as a tool to jump start your client's interest in your high-level services. If this investment is large, then a cost justification may be very necessary to show an attractive return on investment. Formulate a cost justification for your offering and use it as a closing tool with your client.

But how do you formulate cost justification? A formulation will depend on certain factors unique to your offering. These factors may vary from one offering to another. In a service environment, a reduction in labor hours spent to task may be a critical factor in showing a cost savings. How might one calculate a dollar amount? Suppose a company is looking into improving software for automation purposes. Then one may expect a return on investment based on money saved from a reduction in labor hours or machine hours spent to task. You might also add in a dollar amount representing an increase in income due to a new ability to produce more. Let's call this the Z factor.

In some cases, the Z factor may be quite large compared to the savings realized from a reduction in labor hours. In other cases, the reduction in labor hours may be the only source of money. Be sure to use the client's estimated numbers; you as the consultant cannot simply invent estimated numbers. Do this analysis for the first year of the five-year tax window. If a profit is not obvious at the end of the first year, then you will have to do this for each of the five years and back calculate a present value of the return on investment. For information of this kind, consult a finance book. The purpose of this section is simply to get you thinking about how to calculate a return from a given investment. Again, this approach will vary from one situation to another. A detailed analysis is a joint effort by you and your potential customer.

Getting Paid

Now that you have gone to all the trouble of pricing, bidding, and then delivering a job, what about getting paid? One needs to stay on top of accounts receivable. At the outset, establish a sound credit policy. If you are going to take a risk on a client, make it a calculated risk!! Scrutinize their business, study their market, look at their history, and pay them a visit if possible. Working with a client through tough times, with flexible payment terms, can result in a loyal client.

Yet with some clients, you may have to withhold further delivery of service until you get paid. You may request payment up front. Check those credit, customer, and bank references. If your client is late on payments, make a telephone call. If more time elapses with no payment, send a letter indicating possible collection or Small Claims activity. If more time elapses without payment, send a letter indicating definite action.

You may have cash flow problems of your own. Prioritize your debt. For example, take care of your utilities. If you are short of cash, notify your creditors. Inform them of your temporary situation and make a partial payment to everyone you owe; that shows good faith. Give them an idea of how long it will take you to "make good."

The IRS and You

As a consultant, you probably will identify yourself as an independent contractor/proprietor, partnership, or corporation. As an independent contractor/proprietor, you would use a Schedule C to write off your expenses. Depending on how you operate your business, the IRS may or may not agree with your self-declaration as an independent contractor. As a full-time independent contractor/proprietor, you should have income from more than one source, maintain your own office, set your own hours, and provide your own equipment, computers, tools, etc. If you have one major client, the IRS may challenge your independent contractor status and deem you an employee. In this case, you may want to incorporate. Alternatively, you may write into the contract with your client that both parties agree to your service status as an independent contractor. Include clauses that protect your liability.

If you act as an agent whereby you solicit product orders full time for various contractual suppliers for commission, and 80 percent of your time is spent representing one primary contractual supplier, then you may qualify as a statutory employee for that primary supplier. This would allow you to deduct expenses using a Schedule C instead of a Schedule A. Additionally, your "employer" would be deducting and matching part of your paycheck for Social Security and Medicare taxes. Furthermore, up to 20 percent of your time may be spent soliciting business for other contractual suppliers and your place of business could be at your primary supplier's office or at your own office. If the 80-20 percent balance of "time spent" changes to less than 80 percent with a primary supplier and more than 20 percent with secondary suppliers, you would then become, in the eyes of the IRS, a full-time self-employed person. Again, in this case, you would have to provide your own office space.

Remember, the IRS has the final say with interpretation of your status. Consult your business lawyer before signing contracts. You may want to put your contracts together and have your lawyer sign off on their use.

Contractual Relationships

Contractual relationships can take many forms. The following scenario involves one individual, Capable Ed, an independent contractor who is forming a partnership with Tracy Able, who is a recent victim of company downsizing. They wish to obtain a new contract with the company that Tracy Able worked for. A partnership was highly desired by the client company due to a heavy workload. (These clauses are for example only and are not meant to represent complete contracts.)

Partnership Agreement

This Partnership Agreement is entered into and effective as of _____, by: Capable Ed and Tracy Able, the partners.

I. Recitals

1. Business. The partnership will operate as a consulting firm providing services to industry in Northern California. This is a professional or

personal services business which obtains contracts from clients for field services. Tracy Able and Capable Ed will act as consultants for the business.

2. Capable Ed has more than 20 years of successful professional experience. He has operated as an independent consultant for more than 8 years and has contracts with the following clients: ABC Company, DEF Company, etc.

3. Tracy Able has more than 15 years of successful professional experience. She has been an employee with HIJ Company and other companies for more than 6 years. She has 2 years of experience with a major client, KLMNOP Company.

4. Purpose. The partnership was necessary to obtain the contract with KLMNOP Company. The partnership will seek additional favorable contracts with other clients. The partnership will receive and distribute income to the partners; and it will pay certain administrative expenses.

II. Name

The name of the partnership shall be _____.

III. Term

The partnership shall last until terminated as described below.

IV. Contributions

1. Value. The value of the business depends only on the contracts with clients.

2. An acceptable contract will be signed by the partnership no later than _____.

3. Contracts with the following clients will be assigned or legally transferred to the partnership no later than_____.

4. Share. The contributions of the partners is approximately of equal value.

V. Income

1. General. Income shall be divided equally between the two partners except as noted below.

2. Distribution. Income shall be divided and completely distributed to the partners twice per month on the 15th and the last day of each month.

VI. *Administration*

1. Management. Tracy Able shall be the managing partner. She is responsible for administration only as described below.

2. Accounting and Records. The partnership shall maintain client contracts, a checking account, order files, a commission receivable ledge, and other necessary records. The partnership shall provide necessary accounting of income and expenses to each partner.

3. Central Office. The partnership must provide certain central office functions to receive and distribute mail, provide printed letterheads and business cards, and other necessary functions as mutually agreed by the two partners.

4. Allowance. After the first year, that is effective_____, the managing partner, Tracy Able, shall receive an allowance of _____.

VII. *Expenses*

1. Scope. Partnership expenses shall be limited to those incurred by the managing partner, Tracy Able, in carrying out her responsibility for administration as described herein.

2. Share. Partnership expenses shall be shared equally between the two partners.

3. Payment. The managing partner, Tracy Able, shall have an expense account to pay all out-of-pocket partnership expenses. She can be reimbursed or pay directly from the partnership checking account.

4. Assessment. The partners shall make equal payments to the partnership twice per month on the 15th and the last day of each month. The amount shall be determined by mutual agreement of both partners, but must at least cover partnership expenses. Normally, the equal payment can be deducted from income distributions.

5. Individual expenses. Each partner takes care of his or her own expenses.

VIII. *Assets and Liabilities*

The partnership will maintain client contracts, a checking account, and certain other records as described herein. Otherwise, there shall be no partnership property or debt. No partner shall purchase property for the partnership. No partner shall borrow money for the partnership.

IX. *Employees*

There shall be no partnership employees. No partner shall hire a full- or part-time employee unless mutually agreed to by both partners.

X. *Outside Business*

Neither partner shall be a full-time employee of another business. Neither partner shall engage in business in direct competition with the partnership or its clients. Otherwise, either partner may be engaged in one or more other businesses. Neither the partnership nor the other partner shall have any right to the income or profit derived from such other business.

XI. *Termination and Dissolution*

1. Cause. The partnership may be terminated and dissolved immediately and without advanced notice for either of the following causes. B) Partner death or disability. B) Partner full-time employment by another business.

2. Convenience. After the first year, that is effective _____, the partnership may be terminated and dissolved by either partner for any reason with 6 months' advance written notice.

XII. *Ownership Transfer*

1. Value. The value of the partnership business depends only on the contracts with clients. These contracts are for personal services and are neither salable nor transferable.

2. Transfer. Ownership of the partnership business shall not be transferred to third parties.

3. Termination. Upon termination and dissolution of the partnership, one or both partners may retain all or part of the business. That is, one or both partners may obtain one or more contracts with clients. A buy-out agreement may be required to make the separation equitable.

XIII. *Amendments*

This agreement may be amended only by written consent of both partners.

XIV. *General Provisions*

1. State Law. The partners have formed this general partnership under the laws of the State of California, intending to be legally bound thereby.

2. Attachments. Any attached sheet or document shall be regarded as fully contained in this Partnership Agreement.

3. Integration. This Agreement contains the entire understanding of the partners regarding their rights and duties in the partnership. Any alleged oral representations of modifications concerning this Agreement shall be of no force of effect unless contained in a subsequent written modification signed by both partners.

4. Successors. This Agreement shall be binding and for the benefit of the respective successors, inheritors, assigns, and personal representatives of the partners, except to the extent of any contrary provision in the Agreement.

5. Severability. If any term, provision, or condition of this Agreement is held by a court of competent jurisdiction to be invalid, void, or unenforceable, the rest of the Agreement shall remain in full force and effect and shall in no way be affected, impaired, or invalidated.

You may need to disclose confidential information to your client. Here are some clauses that may help safeguard your properties.

Confidential Disclosure Clauses

XYZ Inc. ("XYZ") agrees to disclose to the client indicated below ("Client"), in oral and/or written form, certain information not generally known outside XYZ (the "Information"). In consideration of such disclosure by XYZ, Client agrees as follows:

1. The disclosures relate to XYZ's software development capabilities. The purpose for which the Information is being disclosed is to assist Client in determining the feasibility of implementing XYZ's software development model.

2. The Information is proprietary and confidential to XYZ.

3. Client agrees that the Information furnished by XYZ, which is submitted in writing and marked as "Proprietary Information," or if disclosed orally, is reduced to writing, marked as "Proprietary Information" and submitted within _____ of the original oral disclosure shall be considered Proprietary Information.

4. Client agrees to use the same degree of care to avoid unauthorized dissemination of Proprietary Information as it employs with respect to its own information of a similar nature, which it does not desire to have disseminated.

5. Client agrees that it will not make use of, either directly or indirectly, any of the Information that it receives or has received from Information, other than for the purpose for which the Proprietary Information has been disclosed, except with the specific prior written authorization of an officer of XYZ.

6. Client agrees not to disclose, publish, or otherwise reveal any of the Proprietary Information to any other party, except with the specific prior written authorization of an offer of XYZ.

7. The above restriction will not apply to any information that a) is rightfully known to or in the rightful possession of Client as of the date of its disclosure by XYZ, b) is generally distributed or made available to others by XYZ without restriction as to use or disclosure, c) lawfully becomes known or available to Client from third parties who are not under a similar agreement, directly or indirectly, with XYZ regarding disclosure, or is independently developed by Client, provided the person or persons developing same have not had access to the Proprietary Information.

8. All Information provided in tangible form to Client and any copies of it shall be returned to XYZ at XYZ's request.

(For more information about liability, contracts, and business law, consult *A Legal Road Map for Consultants* by Judy Gedge and published by Oasis Press.)

About Being Organized

Activities in and out of the office should complement each other; the more innovative you are with your office organization, the easier the handling of details will become. In most environments, computer usage is a de facto standard today. Have an alphabetical account file, containing all correspondence between you and your clients. Include in these files all phone notes, letters, names, phone numbers, addresses, technical data, and visit reports. A data base on each customer may be facilitated by the use of good contact management software. In an environment where technical support is critical, electronic mail and Internet use can help you get support from your associates; they also may have the need to get into the data base to add or subtract relevant and needed information. Create a work-in-progress file of action items to be expedited. Shoot for one to two weeks' planning in advance. Use a calendar where you can make a loose three-month plan. It will also give you vision for quarterly plans.

Organization in the Field

When in the field, have your briefcase organized like a mini-desk. As you generate paperwork from the field and as the company generates paperwork for you, the need for a well-organized desk and briefcase to handle this constant flow of records will become obvious. If you do not have a laptop computer (they are expensive), maintain a "black book" or a small multi-ring binder with a print-out of all your accounts alphabetically listed with name, title, address, and phone number for each contact. While in the field, you may call into your office. If you have a message to call Shear Design, Inc., one of your contacts, you'll have their number if the receptionist didn't get it. In addition, keep some kind of daily portable calendar. A cellular phone or pager may be appropriate. A voice mail service can be a great aid.

If you travel by air, get your flights, hotels, and car well in advance. (If you are within three hours by car from your destination, consider driving. It can be more efficient than checking luggage, boarding a plane, and getting another car.) When you arrive, go straight to the car rental counter and get your keys. Then get the luggage you would have had to wait for anyway. Unless a trip is cut and dried, do as much planning for yourself as you can. You need to know what you are getting into and to be aware of any travel alternatives should there be an itinerary change. If you do get bumped off a flight while you are at the airport, go to a pay phone and call the desk or your travel agent's emergency number to make your flight changes in lieu of physically going to that desk and standing in line.

Office Relations

Selling yourself to your co-workers is critical. Unfortunately, inter-office relations are often treated carelessly. This is in part due to the pace and structure of the office environment. Everyone has job responsibilities to carry out in a time-efficient manner; but we can still ask for the expedition of chores politely, and occasionally say "thank you" for a job well done. Be sensitive to everyone's job responsibilities in the office. Share your objectives with everyone so you can have open channels of communication and support coming your way. Use your persuasion skills to help make office decisions. Have empathy for a co-worker's position, even though your position may be quite different. The ability to transcend your own egocentric reality and understand another person's position is important in any teamwork situation.

If there are personnel with negative attitudes in your office environment, do not let them muddy your water. Avoid excessively unproductive chit-chat. If a negatively biased opinion or reaction is solicited from you by another person, whereby you feel that person is trying to "enlist" you, neutralize that person's efforts with a positive word and continue on with your own business. Attempt to generate good, professional work relations. Respect, reward, and empower people. Be consistent. Organize occasional social events.

> *"Those who lose riches lose much, but those who lose courage lose all."*
>
> — UNKNOWN

Summary

1. When you are approaching a large company for the first time, find out how decisions are made and who makes them. Understand the pecking order. Your detective work should come "full circle" with different people saying the same things about what projects are going on relevant to your new business efforts.

2. Assume you are the underdog in competitive situations. Put in writing a client strategy profile to remove any roadblocks for those tough opportunities. By all means, go out on a limb, if you can, in tough situations. Know what the competition is offering and how well you "stack up" against your competitor(s).

3. There are new business opportunities with your existing accounts; they may be growing or planning new projects. Visit your customers — make it easy for them to call you for any help that they might need. Lunch is a very useful tool, whether dealing with new accounts, existing accounts or competitive situations. The frequency and timing of

your lunch invitations are important. Clients may offer information out of the work place they wouldn't offer in the work place.

4. Set up a file system which supports and augments your activities out of the office. Constantly review your goals, forecasts, field plans, and strategies. When in the field, organize your briefcase like a mini-desk. If you travel by air, do as much planning for yourself as you can.

5. Inter-office relations are often neglected. Inform others of your duties and objectives; have support and information coming your way. Use your selling skills to help solve office decisions. Organize occasional social events.

Selling Summary
for Business

Consulting and selling services demands patience, skill, and understanding. Patience, again, because you must invest the time required for the client to accept you and understand the merits of your offering. The skill is required to move the client along to that point.

Be keenly aware of your position, the client's position, and how you affect one another. There are legitimate reasons why people react the way they do. Use your empathy to comprehend the client's position. Ask yourself, "What progress am I making with my client?" Observe and listen carefully to the client's responses to your questions. Don't simply "react" to a client's response. Think about what you are going to say or do next; continually re-evaluate as you proceed with your client. Pay attention to and interpret that non-verbal communication.

It is the critical use of questions that is one of your most valuable selling skills. Questions will give you information to qualify the client. Questions will get you an appointment. Questions will verify the progress you are making with your client. Questions will get you to the right people. Questions will clarify misunderstandings. Questions will maintain the flow and control of information. Questions will imply commitment and ownership. And the final questions, if you have done your job, it is hoped will get you the business.

Depending on the services you offer, you may often use one set of skills one day and another set of skills the next. Hence it is easy to get a little rusty with respect to some of these skills from time to time. Depending on your experience, you may re-read this material several times, review the chapter summaries, or simply review the flow chart. Your profession does require an occasional review of a wide range of skills and continued learning at every level. Insights come over time.

The real challenge is not asking the right kinds of questions, but asking enough of the right kinds of questions. In other words, experienced consultants are almost always asking themselves, "Do I have enough information about this situation?" To help stimulate your creativity to ask those extra questions, you may want to carry around a 3" x 5" card with the following questions:

1. Am I fully aware of the client's understanding of his or her "situation" (which includes an individual's perception of the problem, the need, and the solution) with respect to the offering?

2. Am I aware of the client's perception of how I stack up against the competition and on what that perception is based?

3. Do I know the relationships between all the key players involved in the decision? (This includes the pecking order.)

4. Have I taken the time to write out a client strategy profile (with a deadline date for each activity) for any challenging or complex business situation(s)?

Motivation from Goals

Most of us are successful at attaining goals. However, many professionals lack motivation for further personal and business development. New challenges may still cause anxiety. New challenges, or change in general, kindle our fear of losing security. Don't get in the rut of mastering certain types of challenging situations and hiding from others. It's easy to do. We're very competent, but we procrastinate against new ideas and change because we have to replace comfort with discomfort; we have to go through the same trial and error process to learn and gain control of a new situation. Business is full of changes, and goals development in areas can help push us through the fear of change that exists when confronting new challenges. Work to eliminate anything holding you back from attaining your goals. Don't expect to know all the facts that can influence your goals and their results before you start. Any new information and motivation you generate as you go along, will spur more imagination and creativity for your goal attainment. You will find that as you get more involved with your goals, you will create your own luck. Things will happen to you because you will be looking, motivated, and in the right place at the right time.

Notes

Notes

Index

From The Leading Publisher of Small Business Information
Books that save you time and money.

This authoritative guide will transform the roles of administrators and improve effectiveness for corporate, nonprofit, and community organizations, many of which are over-managed but lack effective leadership. Its skills-oriented solutions teach managers to be effective leaders and train leaders to be better managers — a distinction often overlooked by other management guides.

The Leader's Guide: 15 Essential Skills   **Pages: 250**
Paperback: $19.95   **ISBN: 1-55571-434-X**

Two very practical small business books in one. Book one offers competitive strategies and offers a number of defensive business models that can be adopted, copied, or modified to fit a particular business challenge. Book two, contains fourteen strategies that guarantee sales and profits. Each model contains a competitive strategy that will lessen the impact of a competitor's action by helping target and highly satisfy one specific type of customer.

Navigating the Marketplace   **Pages: 350**
Paperback: $21.95   **ISBN: 1-55571-458-7**

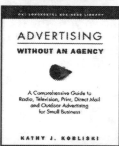

"Advertising," says author Kathy Kobliski, "is not a perfect science. It's not even close." For many small business owners, that means the potential for wasting thousands of dollars on the wrong advertising decisions. This guide is an ideal primer on the in's and out's of advertising and how to get the information you need to pinpoint your advertising objectives. Complete with worksheets, plus help in grasping the lingo, and techniques to target your defined market with the best medium.

Advertising Without An Agency   **Pages: 175**
Paperback: $19.95   **ISBN: 1-55571-429-3**

Surviving Success presents a program for those who wish to lead their companies from promising startup to industry dominance. Meet the challenges of business growth and transition with new insights. Learn from success stories. Be prepared to take proactive steps into your company's next growth transition.

Surviving Success   **Pages: 230**
Paperback: $19.95   **ISBN: 1-55571-446-3**

From The Leading Publisher of Small Business Information
Books that save you time and money.

Today, many corporate CEOs and institutional leaders are advocating a return to liberal arts disciplines — realizing that they lead to better communication skills, a deeper understanding of other players in the global marketplace, and the creativity necessary in any industry to stay competitive. Author Luigi Salvaneschi clearly shows how studying eight specific liberal arts principles can help readers nurture their own leadership skills within and make them an asset for the business world.

Renaissance 2000   **Pages: 300**
Paperback: $22.95   **ISBN: 1-55571-412-9**

Focuses not on prescribing the "best" marketing method, but on using a combination of dozens of marketing techniques, employed by advertising professionals. Teaches the reader how to evaluate many marketing angles, and become better prepared for the challenges of marketing in the new century.

Marketing for the New Millennium   **Pages: 200**
Paperback: $19.95   **ISBN: 1-55571-432-3**

Chock full of proven skills, development tools, applicable to all levels within an organization — this useful guidebook will ensure that your customer service is top-notch. Uncovers the real reasons behind excellent service quality, and how to deploy them in business as a strategic weapon for growth.

Smile Training Isn't Enough   **Pages: 200**
Paperback: $19.95   **ISBN: 1-55571-422-6**

If you can't remember the last time you found yourself smiling at work, it's time to read this book! A refreshing approach to running your business or development within a business. Shows how, where, and why most small business problems occur and what can be done to solve them. Sherlock brings humorous examples from his own business experiences to identify over 45 specific problem areas in business and their easy-to-implement solutions.

Joysticks, Blinking Lights, and Thrills   **Pages: 210**
Paperback: $18.95   **ISBN: 1-55571-401-3**

From The Leading Publisher of Small Business Information
Books that save you time and money.

This all-in-one, easy-to-understand guide will help you get started on the right foot. Packed with valuable start-up information, SmartStart Your (State) Business will prepare you to deal with federal, state, and local regulations imposed on small businesses. This concise, friendly, and up-to-date sourcebook is an affordable investment that details each critical step of starting your own business — from choosing a business structure to writing a top-notch business plan.

SmartStart Your (State) Series **Approx. pages: 325**
Paperback: $19.95 **ISBN: different for each state**

Written by a small business attorney with extensive experience representing consultants. Explains everything a consultant needs to know about the law to properly structure and operate a consulting business. Judy Gedge presents the material in a practical and concrete fashion that answers questions commonly posed by consultants. Also contains a sample consulting agreement, subcontractor's agreement, and a resource directory.

A Legal Road Map for Consultants **Pages: 125**
Paperback: $18.95 **ISBN: 1-55571-460-9**

This sales training guide is specifically for those selling expensive items and interacting face-to-face with consumers. It explains how to employ a winning approach even when stakes are high,and gives insights into patterns of buying exclusive products, so that the seller has a greater sense of comfort through the sales process and exercises more control over its outcome. Author Hal Slater speaks from experience as a three-time recipient of General Motors' highest sales award.

Secrets to High-Ticket Selling **Pages: 200**
Paperback: $19.95 **ISBN: 1-55571-422-6**

Using dozens of real-life examples author Gerald Baron shows how building a relationship is the key to business development and personal fulfillment. By using the book's common-sense principles you can develop strategic relationships that take the concept of "relationship marketing" one step further.

Friendship Marketing **Pages: 230**
Paperback: $18.95 **ISBN: 1-55571-399-8**

ALL MAJOR CREDIT CARDS ACCEPTED

CALL TO PLACE AN ORDER
— or —
TO RECEIVE A FREE CATALOG **1-800-228-2275**

International Orders (541) 479-9464 *Fax Orders* (541) 476-1479
Web site http://www.psi-research.com *Email* sales@psi-research.com

PSI Research P.O. Box 3727 Central Point, Oregon 97502 U.S.A.

Order Directly From **The Oasis Press**®

Call, Mail, Email, or Fax Your Order to: PSI Research, P.O. Box 3727, Central Point, OR 97502
Order Phone USA & Canada: +1 800 228-2275   Email: sales@psi-research.com   Fax: +1 541 476-1479

Includes
Titles Through
Winter 1999

TITLE	✔ BINDER	✔ PAPERBACK	QUANTITY	COST
Advertising Without An Agency: A Comprehensive Guide to Radio, Television, Print...		❑ $19.95		
Bottom Line Basics: Understand and Control Your Finances	❑ $39.95	❑ $19.95		
BusinessBasics: A Microbusiness Startup Guide		❑ $16.95		
The Business Environmental Handbook	❑ $39.95	❑ $19.95		
Business Owner's Guide to Accounting & Bookkeeping		❑ $19.95		
businessplan.com: how to write a web-woven strategic business plan		❑ $19.95		
Buyer's Guide to Business Insurance	❑ $39.95	❑ $19.95		
California Corporation Formation Package		❑ $29.95		
Collection Techniques for a Small Business	❑ $39.95	❑ $19.95		
A Company Policy and Personnel Workbook	❑ $49.95	❑ $29.95		
Company Relocation Handbook	❑ $39.95	❑ $19.95		
CompControl: The Secrets of Reducing Workers' Compensation Costs	❑ $39.95	❑ $19.95		
Complete Book of Business Forms		❑ $19.95		
Connecting Online: Creating a Successful Image on the Internet		❑ $21.95		
Customer Engineering: Cutting Edge Selling Strategies	❑ $39.95	❑ $19.95		
Develop & Market Your Creative Ideas		❑ $15.95		
Developing International Markets: Shaping Your Global Presence		❑ $19.95		
Doing Business in Russia: Basic Facts for the Pioneering Entrepreneur		❑ $19.95		
Draw The Line: A Sexual Harassment Free Workplace		❑ $17.95		
Entrepreneurial Decisionmaking: A Survival Manual for the Next Millennium		❑ $21.95		
The Essential Corporation Handbook		❑ $21.95		
The Essential Limited Liability Company Handbook	❑ $39.95	❑ $21.95		
Export Now: A Guide for Small Business	❑ $39.95	❑ $24.95		
Financial Decisionmaking: A CPA/Attorney's Perspective		❑ $19.95		
Financial Management Techniques for Small Business	❑ $39.95	❑ $19.95		
Financing Your Small Business: Techniques for Planning, Acquiring, & Managing Debt		❑ $19.95		
Franchise Bible: How to Buy a Franchise or Franchise Your Own Business	❑ $39.95	❑ $24.95		
Friendship Marketing: Growing Your Business by Cultivating Strategic Relationships		❑ $18.95		
Funding High-Tech Ventures		❑ $21.95		
Home Business Made Easy		❑ $19.95		
Information Breakthrough: How to Turn Mountains of Confusing Data into Gems of Useful Information		❑ $22.95		
Improving Staff Productivity: Ideas to Increase Profits		❑ $16.95		
The Insider's Guide to Small Business Loans		❑ $19.95		
InstaCorp – Incorporate In Any State (Book & Software)		❑ $29.95		
Joysticks, Blinking Lights and Thrills		❑ $18.95		
Keeping Score: An Inside Look at Sports Marketing		❑ $18.95		
Know Your Market: How to Do Low-Cost Market Research	❑ $39.95	❑ $19.95		
The Leader's Guide: 15 Essential Skills		❑ $19.95		
Legal Expense Defense: How to Control Your Business' Legal Costs and Problems	❑ $39.95	❑ $19.95		
Legal Road Map for Consultants		❑ $18.95		
Location, Location, Location: How to Select the Best Site for Your Business		❑ $19.95		
Mail Order Legal Guide	❑ $45.00	❑ $29.95		
Managing People: A Practical Guide		❑ $21.95		
Marketing for the New Millennium: Applying New Techniques		❑ $19.95		
Marketing Mastery: Your Seven Step Guide to Success	❑ $39.95	❑ $19.95		
The Money Connection: Where and How to Apply for Business Loans and Venture Capital	❑ $39.95	❑ $24.95		
Moonlighting: Earn a Second Income at Home		❑ $15.95		
Navigating the Marketplace: Growth Strategies For Your Business		❑ $21.95		
No Money Down Financing for Franchising		❑ $19.95		
People Investment: How to Make Your Hiring Decisions Pay Off For Everyone	❑ $39.95	❑ $19.95		
Power Marketing for Small Business	❑ $39.95	❑ $19.95		
Profit Power: 101 Pointers to Give Your Business a Competitive Edge		❑ $19.95		
Proposal Development: How to Respond and Win the Bid	❑ $39.95	❑ $21.95		
Public Relations Marketing: Making a Splash Without Much Cash		❑ $19.95		
Raising Capital: How to Write a Financing Proposal		❑ $19.95		
Renaissance 2000: Liberal Arts Essentials for Tomorrow's Leaders		❑ $22.95		
Retail in Detail: How to Start and Manage a Small Retail Business		❑ $15.95		
Secrets of High Ticket Selling		❑ $19.95		
Secrets to Buying and Selling a Business		❑ $24.95		
Secure Your Future: Financial Planning at Any Age	❑ $39.95	❑ $19.95		
Selling Services: A Guide for the Consulting Professional		❑ $18.95		
The Small Business Insider's Guide to Bankers		❑ $18.95		
BOOK SUB-TOTAL (Additional titles on other side)				

TITLE	✔ BINDER	✔ PAPERBACK	QUANTITY	COST
SmartStart Your (State) Business... series		❑ $19.95		
Please specify which state(s) you would like:				
Smile Training Isn't Enough: The Three Secrets to Excellent Customer Service		❑ $19.95		
Start Your Business (Also available as a book and disk package, see below)		❑ $ 9.95 *(without disk)*		
Successful Business Plan: Secrets & Strategies	❑ $49.95	❑ $27.95		
Successful Network Marketing for The 21st Century		❑ $15.95		
Surviving Success: Managing the Challenges of Growth		❑ $19.95		
TargetSmart! Database Marketing for the Small Business		❑ $19.95		
Top Tax Saving Ideas for Today's Small Business		❑ $16.95		
Twenty-One Sales in a Sale: What Sales Are You Missing?		❑ $19.95		
Which Business? Help in Selecting Your New Venture		❑ $18.95		
Write Your Own Business Contracts		❑ $24.95		
BOOK SUB-TOTAL (Don't forget to include your amount from the previous side)				

OASIS SOFTWARE   Please specify which computer operating system you use (DOS, Mac OS, or Windows)

TITLE	✔ Windows	✔ Mac OS	QUANTITY	COST
California Corporation Formation Package ASCII Software	❑ $ 39.95	❑ $ 39.95		
Company Policy & Personnel Software Text Files	❑ $ 49.95	❑ $ 49.95		
Financial Management Techniques (Full Standalone)	❑ $ 99.95			
Financial Templates	❑ $ 69.95	❑ $ 69.95		
The Insurance Assistant Software (Full Standalone)	❑ $ 29.95			
Start Your Business (Software for Windows™)	❑ $ 19.95			
Successful Business Plan (Software for Windows™)	❑ $ 99.95			
Successful Business Plan Templates	❑ $ 69.95	❑ $ 69.95		
The Survey Genie - Customer Edition (Full Standalone)	❑ $199.95 (WIN)	❑ $149.95 (DOS)		
The Survey Genie - Employee Edition (Full Standalone)	❑ $199.95 (WIN)	❑ $149.95 (DOS)		
Winning Business Plans in Color (MS Office Addition)	❑ $ 39.95			
SOFTWARE SUB-TOTAL				

BOOK & DISK PACKAGES Please specify which computer operating system you use (DOS, Mac OS, or Windows)

TITLE	✔ Windows	✔ MacOS	✔ Binder	✔ Paperback	QUANTITY	COST
The Buyer's Guide to Business Insurance w/ Insurance Assistant	❑		❑ $ 59.95	❑ $ 39.95		
California Corporation Formation Book & Text Files	❑	❑		❑ $ 59.95		
Company Policy & Personnel Book & Software Text Files	❑	❑	❑ $ 89.95	❑ $ 69.95		
Financial Management Techniques Book & Software	❑		❑ $129.95	❑ $ 119.95		
Start Your Business Paperback & Software (Software for Windows™)	❑			❑ $ 24.95		
Successful Business Plan Book & Software for Windows™	❑		❑ $125.95	❑ $109.95		
Successful Business Plan Book & Software Templates	❑	❑	❑ $109.95	❑ $ 89.95		
BOOK & DISK PACKAGE SUB-TOTAL						

SOLD TO: Please give street address for shipping.

Name:

Title:

Company:

Street Address:

City/State/Zip:

Daytime Phone: Email:

SHIP TO: If different than above, please give alternate street address

Name:

Company:

Street Address:

City/State/Zip:

Daytime Phone:

GRAND TOTAL

SUB-TOTALS *(from other side)*	$
SUB-TOTALS *(from this side)*	$
SHIPPING (see chart below)	$
TOTAL ORDER	**$**

If your purchase is:	Shipping costs within the USA:
$0 - $25	$5.00
$25.01 - $50	$6.00
$50.01 - $100	$7.00
$100.01 - $175	$9.00
$175.01 - $250	$13.00
$250.01 - $500	$18.00
$500.01 +	4% of total merchandise

**You can also order online
24-hours a day and 7 days a week at
http://www.psi-research.com**

PAYMENT INFORMATION: *Rush service is available, call for details.*
International and Canadian Orders: *Please call 1-541-479-9464 for quote on shipping.*
Please indicate a method of payment below:

❑ **CHECK** Enclosed, payable to PSI Research   ❑ **VISA**   ❑ **MASTERCARD**   ❑ **AMEX**   ❑ **DISCOVER**

Card Number: Expires:

Signature: Name On Card:

Stay Up-To-Date! Register your copy and stay current with the latest information and product releases from The Oasis Press®

Please answer these questions to let us know how our products are working for you, and what we could do to serve you better.

Selling Services

Rate this product's overall quality of information:
☐ Excellent
☐ Good
☐ Fair
☐ Poor

Rate the quality of printed materials:
☐ Excellent
☐ Good
☐ Fair
☐ Poor

Rate the format:
☐ Excellent
☐ Good
☐ Fair
☐ Poor

Did the product provide what you needed?
☐ Yes ☐ No

If not, what should be added?
_____
_____
_____
_____
_____
_____
_____
_____
_____
_____

This product is:
☐ Clear and easy to follow
☐ Too complicated
☐ Too elementary

Were the worksheets easy to use?
☐ Yes ☐ No ☐ N/A

Should we include?
☐ More worksheets
☐ Fewer worksheets
☐ No worksheets

How do you feel about the price?
☐ Lower than expected
☐ About right
☐ Too expensive

How many employees are in your company?
☐ Self-employed
☐ Under 10 employees
☐ 10 - 50 employees
☐ 51 - 99 employees
☐ 100 - 250 employees
☐ Over 250 employees

How many people in the city your company is in?
☐ 50,000 - 100,000
☐ 100,000 - 500,000
☐ 500,000 - 1,000,000
☐ Over 1,000,000
☐ Rural (Under 50,000)

What is your type of business?
☐ Retail
☐ Service
☐ Consultant
☐ Contractor/Freelance
☐ Internet Related
☐ Government
☐ Manufacturer
☐ Distributor
☐ Other: _____
_____

What is your position in the company?
(please check one)
☐ Owner
☐ Administrative
☐ Sales/Marketing
☐ Creative
☐ Internet related
☐ Finance
☐ Human resources
☐ Production
☐ Operations
☐ Computer/MIS

How did you learn about this product?
☐ From a friend
☐ Used in a seminar or class
☐ The Oasis Press®
☐ Received a mailing
☐ Saw in bookstore
☐ Saw in library
☐ Saw review in:
  ☐ Newspaper
  ☐ Magazine
  ☐ Radio/TV

Where did you buy this product?
☐ Catalog
☐ Major bookstore
☐ Small, local bookstore
☐ Office supply store
☐ Educational bookstore
☐ Online
☐ Other: _____

Are you connected to the Internet?
☐ Yes ☐ No

If yes, on what type of computer system?
☐ Macintosh
☐ Windows
☐ UNIX
☐ Other: _____

If yes, what is your primary use of the Internet?
☐ Web surfing
☐ Email
☐ Shopping online
☐ Statistical information
☐ Chatting
☐ Other: _____

What do you primarily use your computer for?
☐ Word processing
☐ Accounting/Payroll
☐ Spreadsheet
☐ Inventory
☐ Order processing
☐ Design/Graphics
☐ Database
☐ Scheduling
☐ Internet/Intranet
☐ Network Admin.
☐ Don't use a computer
☐ Other: _____
_____

May we call you to follow up or use your comments for our marketing materials?
☐ Yes ☐ No

May we add your name to our mailing list? ☐ Yes ☐ No

Thank You. For more information about The Oasis Press®, be sure to check out our Web site at http://www.psi-research.com

Just fill in your name and address here, fold (see back), and mail.

Name _____

Title _____

Company _____

Phone _____

Address _____

City/State/Zip _____

Email Address (Home) _____

(Business) _____

12/98

If you have friends or associates who might appreciate receiving our catalogs, please list here.

Name_____   Name_____

Title_____   Title_____

Company_____   Company_____

Phone_____   Phone_____

Address_____   Address_____

Address_____   Address_____

FOLD HERE FIRST

NO POSTAGE
NECESSARY
IF MAILED
IN THE
UNITED STATES

BUSINESS REPLY MAIL

FIRST CLASS MAIL PERMIT NO. 002 MERLIN, OREGON

POSTAGE WILL BE PAID BY ADDRESSEE

PSI Research
PO BOX 1414
Merlin OR 97532-9900

FOLD HERE SECOND, THEN TAPE TOGETHER

Please cut
along this
vertical line,
fold twice,
tape together
and mail.